TO: T / unn

MW00768259

THE BOYS OF ENON ROAD

⟫ summer of 1968 ⟪

ALLAN THAMES

Allan Thames
2007
Douglas County
courthouse

TATE PUBLISHING & *Enterprises*

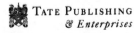

TATE PUBLISHING
& Enterprises

The Boys of Enon Road
Copyright © 2006 by Allan Thames. All rights reserved.

Scripture quotations marked "NIV" are taken from the *Holy Bible, New International Version* ®, Copyright © 1973, 1978, 1984 by International Bible Society. Used by permission of Zondervan Publishing House. All rights reserved.

This novel is a work of fiction. Names, descriptions, entities and incidents included in the story are products of the author's imagination. Any resemblance to actual persons, events and entities is entirely coincidental.

Book design copyright © 2006 by Tate Publishing, LLC. All rights reserved.
Cover design by Rusty Eldred
Interior design by Lynly Taylor

Published in the United States of America

ISBN: 1–5988654–7-1
06.08.01

THE BOYS OF ENON ROAD

DEDICATION

The Boys of Enon Road is lovingly dedicated to my mother, who would lay down with me for my afternoon naps as a child and tell me stories that fired my imagination. She would then listen patiently as I made up my own stories. She is still reading my stories today. It is also dedicated to "The Boys."

CONTENTS

One . . . . Kings and Emperors 9

Two . . . . Pandora's Box 13

Three . . . . School Is Out 27

Four . . . . A Disappointing Afternoon 35

Five . . . . Lightning Strike? 43

Six . . . . Downtown 49

Seven . . . . Dogs 53

Eight . . . . Dickie Drops the Ball 57

Nine . . . . Death 67

Ten . . . . Dickie Goes to a Campout 71

Eleven . . . . The Bambino Strikes 77

Twelve . . . . Moby Bass 97

Thirteen . . . . The New Ball Field 101

Fourteen . . . . The Legacy 109

Fifteen . . . . VBS 115

Sixteen . . . . Hill No. 121 121

Seventeen . . . . Down Strawberry Mountain . . . 127

Eighteen . . . . Deacons and Preachers 135

Nineteen . . . . Muscadine Vines 143

Twenty . . . . Moby Strikes 147

Twenty-One . . . . . . Innocence 159

CHAPTER ONE

⇒ *Kings and Emperors* ⇐

The days lived along quiet, country Enon Road, about 30 miles west and south of Atlanta, by my cousins and me during that long, hot, thundery summer of 1968 were days of living like kings and emperors, lords of all we saw and of every acre we roamed. They were days of doing as we pleased, as long as we pleased (as long as our mommas pleased). They were long days, from early sun up with dew on the ground, to late sundown with dew back on the ground; days of playing baseball under the blue sky and blazing sun, and days of fishing under the blue sky and blazing sun; days of playing army in the chigger laden woods and pine thickets; days of building huts out of dead pine limbs under the wild plum bushes while we kept a wary out eye out for snakes; days of riding bikes without fenders that would splash mud on your back should you ride through a mud puddle on the many days there were mud puddles; and days of just sitting around talking, or arguing, or wrestling, if that was what we wanted to do.

Those were the glory days. They were days of innocence; the days before the yearnings and stirrings of early manhood; days when everything was simple and easy. They were days when there were no girls around and few thoughts about girls to complicate life. There was no worrying about the opposite sex, or even thinking about sex, or wondering about "it" at all. Not until one of the cousins stole his dad's "Playboy" did we even realize or think how boys and girls were different. Cousin Little Dickie even showed up with a stag magazine at a campout we had. It was a magazine that not only showed it all but told about it all in graphic detail. I had had no idea! Little Dickie and I went out fishing in the lake behind the house that evening. I was in one end of the boat, and Little Dickie was in the other. He was trying desperately to hang onto to a fishing pole and the magazine—trying to fish and read and look all at the same time. Things really got complicated when the sun went down and he was trying to use a flashlight to see all those pictures and read those stories. I am not sure what would have happened if he had caught a fish, but I believe the magazine would have been saved at all costs. It would still be some years, however, before we cared too much about that kind of stuff. Kids seemed to mature slower in those days. Right then "it" was curiosity rather than lust. I never figured out how my cousin, having just turned twelve years old, came into possession of that magazine. In our more modern and enlightened society, all any child has to have access to is the internet or cable television (and parents who don't supervise what they watch). That child will be bombarded with graphic sexual images that would have been considered pornography on Enon Road in 1968, and still should be.

To us back then in those uncomplicated, calmer days, life was a bicycle and miles of open, flat road with no cars or cares on it. Life was a fishing pole with a Zebco 33 reel attached with 15 lb test line and hours and hours to fish. Life was floating lazily along in the boat, watching turtles sun themselves on the logs and stumps that stuck out of the water. Life was a baseball game in the late afternoon when the sun's rays were not so bright in your eyes, and there was a hint of the promised cooler evening to come. Life was an ice cold, six-ounce Coca Cola drunk slowly in the shade of an old elm tree after cutting the acre or so of Aunt Alma's yard with a push mower in the heat of the day. Life was up early, out the door, and into the woods to run, rip, shout, and fight imaginary enemies or each other. Life was eating ice cream, watermelon, and grilled out hotdogs and hamburgers and watching or playing baseball on the Fourth of July. Life was simple. You made no long-term plans and didn't know nor care what commitment meant. You had no schedule to keep (other than being close by when Mom called you in to lunch or supper). You had no place to be and no time to be there. You took each day as it came. You didn't know you were doing it, but you were still living life to the fullest. You ran hard from the moment you left the house with the screen door flapping behind you in the morning, until the last light of day left the sky when Mom called you in, dirty, nasty, sweaty, filthy and tired, but happy. Oh, just to live those carefree days one more time when terrible things like death were unknown to us; when hospitals were for birthing babies or having your tonsils removed. In those days, everything we needed was provided because we didn't need much besides food, an occasional patch for our flat bike tires, and maybe a new baseball. I wish we could live without visits to the funeral homes and cemeteries with an ever increasing frequency. I want to live not facing sickness; to live thinking I will never grow old; to live without fear of Alzheimer's, stroke, heart attack or cancer; to live without the accompanying pains of aging like arthritis or aggravations of failing eyesight; to live without worrying about my weight or diet. I want to live without taking blood pressure medicine or pills for this ailment or that ailment; to live without financial stress and family crisis; to live looking forward only to the next meal, the next game, or the next fishing excursion. Life was like that for the boys of Enon Road in the summer of 1968.

CHAPTER TWO

⋙ *Pandora's Box* ⋘

You can't be young again. You can never regain lost youth. You can never walk those trails or ride those roads again with the same attitude and outlook on life as you once had. You can try to hide your age, but you can only do that for so long. You can't roll the years back or freeze time. Only in youth can you have that innocence of evil, sin, lust, hatred, or meanness. Once that innocence is gone, like those evils fleeing Pandora's box, you can never have it back. You can never feel the same way about life again. I was either very innocent or extremely naïve as I approached my teenage years. Those were the years when the innocence or naiveté finally would be gone forever. Only now, in my later life, do I long to return to those days. I grieve that I cannot find that lost innocence, for the experience of my years has made me calloused and hard. There was so much evil going on out in the wide world that I had never encountered or heard about as I lived on Enon Road in 1968. But I would learn about it all whether I wanted to or not.

In those early days, I had not heard anything about some of the hot-button issues of today. I had no concept of and had never heard of homosexuality. I had heard about Sodom and Gomorrah, of course, but to that point in life, I had never understood why God had gotten so mad and destroyed those cities. Sex was something I never heard mentioned or discussed in the living room, the bedroom, or on the television. If it had been, I would have rushed out of the room in embarrassment. Up until then, most of the television characters we watched had separate beds, so the thoughts would never even come to mind. When someone was pregnant, she was said to be "expecting." When her baby was born, if she nursed (which was rare in those days), she did it discreetly in a back bedroom, out of sight. Sex education was not taught until the seventh grade, and then you had to have a permission slip signed by your parents. A doctor would come in and talk to the boys, and his nurse would talk to the girls. My discussion on the birds and the bees was still many months away. That day marked, to some, the coming of age, the loss of innocence when you began to learn serious things about the adult world and your own changing body. The doctor would teach us words like "rape," "venereal disease" ("VD" was what he called it), "period," "puberty," "intercourse," and many other words that I had never heard before over on Enon Road. Much of what he said made me swear to stay away from girls forever. When I saw Little Dickie's magazine a few weeks after this frank discussion, I began putting two and two together. Even then, it was a long time before I added it up to make four.

Maybe we were just ignorant. If so, then we were even more ignorant of the world events swirling around us. We had no idea what all the race riots we saw on television were about, what all the black protestors wanted, who Martin Luther King, Jr. was, or why he had been shot earlier that year in April. I know that when it was reported that night on the news, Mom rushed to lock the doors with fear on her face as she pulled out Dad's shotgun and loaded it. Our world was not black and white like our television; our world was only white because we had little exposure to black people in our area. In those days, blacks lived in black neighborhoods, and whites lived in white neighborhoods, like many areas today. Blacks went to black churches, and whites went to white churches. Our church board of deacons held serious discussions about what to do if a black person actually came to church. Today they hold discussions as to how to get black folks to come to that church. There was a small part of a nearby community where a concentration of poor, black people lived that we called "Nigger Town." We called it that not out of meanness or trying to make it a racial epithet, but because that was just what we had heard adults call black people and that poor part of town, particularly. Now people refer to it as the "N" word as if it is the worst cuss word ever uttered. When one considers the hatred, racism, and prejudice that lives behind that word, then you realize how bad it really is.

"White flight" was the term given when a black family bought into a white neighborhood and suddenly all the houses on the block were for sale. Almost over-night, where white faces had been cutting the grass, now black ones could be seen doing the yard work—not for some white owner but in their own yards. Some real estate people were said to have made fortunes by buying one home in a white neighborhood for an exorbitant price, placing a black family in it, then canvassing the neighbor-hood and enlisting others who were ready to sell because "blacks had moved in." We wondered what was so bad about black people that whites were afraid to live beside them. The rumor was that once a black moved into your area, the value of your property would fall, so everyone was anxious to get out before that happened. I remember when there was a rumor of a black child coming to Cliftondale Elementary School, which never happened when I was there. We were told that it was fine to be friends with blacks. We should talk with them at school and treat them like white folks. We were also told that we shouldn't consider bringing them home or staying at their homes overnight. It was like they were aliens from Mars or something worse. Discrimination and racial hatred are not inborn. They are taught, passed down from generation to generation. One wonders when that cycle will be broken, when both white people and black people will stop teaching their children to hate the other.

The boys of Enon Road didn't hate black people. The only black people we knew were the maids that came in once a week to help with laundry. We loved them, and they loved, respected, and appreciated us. But by 1968, their employment by our families had almost ended. In our earlier days on Enon Road, three of our families shared one maid. Until I went to high school, Della and Lottie were the only black people I knew, so how could I hate them? They came in and ironed our clothes, but we were taught to respect them like we respected anyone and everyone else. They appreciated the opportunity to work for us white folks, and our families appreciated them doing it. What was all the fuss about, anyway? The boys of Enon Road didn't understand the marches, sit-ins, demonstrations, and riots in the cities, or why black people were being beaten and jailed. I had no idea there were separate schools for black and white kids. I did not know that at one time, blacks could not eat in some restaurants, could not use the same water fountains or restrooms, could not live where they wanted, had to ride in the back of buses, and made lower salaries than their white counterparts. We knew and cared nothing for all of that. It was adult politics and did not come any further into our lives than the living room where the black and white television sat. I guess it should have been white and black television. Whites always came first in our society, and there were few blacks on television other than "Amos and Andy" reruns, which we loved. I did know that I saw both white and black soldiers in Vietnam fighting together on the television news. I guess some of them were fighting for a freedom back home that did not really exist; a freedom that when they returned was still denied to them; a freedom so narrow that a black man who had fought bravely alongside his white comrades in Vietnam still could not go in the front door of some establishments back home in Georgia.

The Vietnam War was swirling in the background as we played in the woods that summer. It was on the television news every night. Walter Cronkite or David Brinkley and Chet Huntley reported the scores for the day. Watching them report on body counts was like watching sports reporters. "Today, there were reports of 136 Viet Cong killed and 31 Americans." That meant we won the day 136–31. At least that is how we kids understood it. It was like a score from a football game—Atlanta Falcons 28, Green Bay Packers 10. Every night we were amazed at the fighting for various hills. "The Viet Cong recaptured Hill No. 121 today," Cronkite would report, "after the American forces had recaptured it only yesterday." In other words, we had lost that day. But the next morning, we boys would head out to the woods, recapture Hill

17

No. 121 ourselves, and only give it back when going in for lunch. The war had no meaning to us because it was so far away, but young men not too much older than us were dying. Lots of young men were dying or being maimed, their bodies being shattered in real life combat where their buddies were crying and cursing around them. Our mailman's son went off to the war, and one morning at breakfast, Mom and Dad talked in hushed tones about the boy's death on Hill No. 121. Each dead soldier, marine, or airman seemed just part of the daily body count to news reporters, but that one young man was someone very real and tangible to Mom and Dad. They had vague memories of World War II but had very real memories of the Korean War. Dad especially remembered Korea, as he served there in Graves Registration. He knew first hand what body counts were all about, and how real the death in war really is. He knew and understood morgues and toe tags and knew why servicemen wore dog tags. In our wars in the woods with unseen Viet Cong or Communists, when we got "killed," we would always jump up and say, "I'm another man," but that could not happen in Vietnam—not for our mailman's son. But we did not understand that in our age of innocence.

1968 was a violent year with the U.S.S. Pueblo, an admitted spy ship, being captured by the North Koreans in late January. It was followed a week later by the North Vietnamese starting the Tet Offensive and capturing Saigon for a while, killing lots of our young men in the process. That attack showed people back in the U.S. that the war could not be won. The boys of Enon Road, who still fought the War Between the States in the woods occasionally, were not surprised by the fact that once again,

Northern aggressors were causing trouble for decent, peace loving Southerners. The violence continued with the My Lai massacre in the little Vietnamese village in March, Martin Luther King, Jr. being murdered in April, Robert Kennedy being gunned down on June 5th, and raging demonstrations at the August Democratic Presidential Convention in Chicago. During the convention, demonstrators were beaten and arrested by the police, and not necessarily in that order. It was no wonder that neither Hubert Humphrey nor Richard Nixon won a mandate in the November election. With all the troubles in their world, adults were ready for a change, so more voted for Nixon. Our parents discussed these and other issues, but they didn't mean much to us boys, though I had heard of Nixon and hoped he would be president because I just did not like the name "Hubert" nor "Humphrey."

In the Bible, Romans 16:19 (NIV) says, ". . . . be wise about what is good and innocent about what is evil." Even with all that violence raging in the outside world, the boys of Enon Road were just about as innocent of evil as Adam and Eve had been in the garden before the snake and apple thing that we learned about in Vacation Bible School. Not that we were perfect; it was just that we had not been exposed to the evil and meanness in the world. Not really; not beyond our television. Not on Enon Road—not yet. Evil men or lude women, murderers, whoremongers, drunkards, idolaters, adulterers, those guilty of licentiousness (or any of those Biblically evil people that our minister preached against) did not wander into our territory on Enon Road in 1968. I couldn't tell you today what licentiousness is or if I need to be forgiven for it. I have a good idea about whoremongering, and am sure I am not guilty of that. I wasn't sure what whoremongering was in 1968 because I had never heard the word "whore." (In our world, "bitch" meant female dog, and a "son of a bitch" was a male puppy. That is how Uncle Gene explained it when Aunt Lois heard him say it in front of us once.) We did live in a different world, in a different time, in a different place. It was a place where homes were not burglarized and people were not murdered. The only drugs sold on our streets were those delivered by the local Rexal Drug Store when someone was sick. I remember the delivery services we had in those days. The Ben Hill drug store would deliver Cheracol when you had a cough, or Paregoric (we didn't know it had morphine in it) when you had a bellyache. The bread man came every week to deliver fresh bread and sometimes even cookies. In the early days, the milk man delivered milk in glass bottles before changing over to plastic jugs (which were great for running trot lines in the lake when they were empty). Sometimes, Mom splurged and bought chocolate milk—really deep, dark, delicious, almost frozen chocolate milk. We even had a Charles Chips potato chip man that delivered chips in a gallon-sized, round tin. Every week you would give him the empty tin, and he would replace it with a full one. Those were the days before pizza delivery, which was just as well because we didn't eat pizza in our house.

Those were simpler times. It may well have been that innocence and simplicity had ended everywhere else in America except on Enon Road by 1968. Now that I think back on it, it may have been that that innocence and simplicity had ended everywhere else and in everyone else but me by that time. I was living a shielded life. I ignored or didn't care about anything but baseball, fishing, and anything else that pleased me. I know now that innocence had ended in my cousins by then. They were exposed to things in their homes that I had no clue about since they never brought those things outside with them. I never knew about Uncle Gene's alcoholism. I never knew that he beat on Brad, his stepson. I never knew about the terrible arguments Gene had with Aunt Lois when he was drunk. Some people get mellow or happy when they get drunk, so I have learned. Uncle Gene obviously got mean, and when he got mean he hit people. Brad was his most obvious target because he was smaller. Gene never hit Aunt Lois, even when drunk, because he was afraid of her. Cowardice is a character trait in most abusive fathers, so Uncle Gene picked his targets—the young and the vulnerable, the ones who could not hit back or walk out. Now that Brad is into his second marriage, is the father of 5 kids with 3 different women, can't hold a job, and is an alcoholic himself, I begin to realize why. I have seen Brad almost drunk, getting belligerent and mean, and I know he has hit his kids. I also watched many years later as Brad struggled down the aisle at church, shaking violently from the DT's, his life in ruins, as he gave his heart to the Lord. He was baptized, still shaking, in the little country church we attended in 1968. Brad lived a vicious cycle, started with alcohol, perpetuated by alcohol. My grandpa drank, though only in moderation, not more than one beer when he got home at night. Gene drank to excess, and later on so did Brad. Grandpa controlled his drinking, but Gene and Brad could not. I cannot comprehend why our society tolerates anything like alcohol that causes so much heartache, pain, and so much damage to be inflicted on the innocent. I can't understand why drunk drivers are not put in prison for life, especially the repeat offenders. I cannot understand why beer commercials are permitted on television if hard liquor commercials are not. Beer and hard liquor both kill people. We condemn cigarette smoking but not drinking, and that is hypocritical. Smoking a normal cigarette never led anyone to physically abuse a child or to kill someone while driving. Brad said nothing about his pain, and we never knew about it until many, many years later.

The rest of us boys never knew about the marital conflicts that Aunt Vivian and Uncle Richard were having in Grandma and Grandpa's house, either. It was not something their boys brought to the front yard ball games, the biking marathons, the wars in the woods, the building of huts, or the camping trips. Those adventures were their escapes from reality. Their escapes were my reality. My life was nothing but the daily adventures to be looked forward to for the sheer enjoyment of them. For the cousins, the adventures were their opportunities to get away from the nearly constant in-house warfare. They were the chance to just be kids doing kid things and to get away from the nasty world their adults were creating. The adventures let Brad get away from his dad's hammerings, and Aunt Vivian's boys could get away from the bickering.

I think Aunt Vivian always wanted more than she had. She wanted to be more than she really was. I am told that what you don't have at age 10 or 12 is what you spend the rest of your life trying to obtain. It may be that she was dirt poor at that age and as an adult, she wanted to have the nice things in life that she had been denied as a child. She wasn't happy that Richard was a mechanic.

She knew that on mechanic's wages they were never going to be able to go exotic places and do exotic things like living out romantic fantasies. In fact, Uncle Richard was not into all of that exotic, romantic stuff, anyway. He was into and focused only on building and rebuilding motors, engines, starters, alternators, and anything that had to do with a car. I think the little shop he had behind the house was his escape from reality, his refuge from having to face his wife and deal with her or their emotionally disturbed son, Stevie. Uncle Richard had the permanently grease-stained hands of an honest, hard working mechanic. After awhile, Aunt Vivian couldn't stand the thought of those hands touching her. She couldn't stand the thought of living the rest of her life without the romance she found in the novels she read, and she couldn't stand the thought of not experiencing wealth and all the leisure, excitement, and opportunity it brings. Since she was miserable, she made all those around her miserable. If she had loved cars more, and he had tried to romance her once in awhile, they might have made it. But Aunt Vivian knew nothing about cars, and as much as Uncle Richard knew about car engines, he did not understand the finer art of romancing women. Years later after her eventual divorce from Uncle Richard, she married and divorced a succession of rich men and finally had her money. Whether she found happiness or not, I do not know. Uncle Richard married a rich lady of his own who was content to provide him with enough of an allowance to spend all the time he wanted working on cars. She did not mind his grease-stained hands at all.

Aunt Vivian's three boys never talked about their home life. Our families all had a rule that what went on in the house, stayed in the house. Little Dickie was her oldest, almost a year younger than me. We were so close to each other in age that we had a sibling rivalry even though we were just first cousins. We were like brothers. With such a close relationship, we often clashed. Being the oldest of our gang, I was a little bit bigger than him, and so I was the natural leader. I always hit the ball a little farther, caught bigger or more fish, won every bike race and footrace, and was always just a little bit better in everything we did together. He resented it and never accepted it. We had our share of scraps, fights and tussles, but we never remembered them longer than one day. Once the sun went down, so did our wrath. It was too bad his parents didn't live the same way. We had our share of verbal assaults, pushes, shoves, and name calling through the years, but for some reason, in that final, wonderful summer, we argued or fought very little. It may have been that he realized that I was about to outgrow the group, and that his turn at leadership was right around the corner. He may have understood that I was maturing and allowing him to win a few races, and I wasn't being as bossy in my leadership. Maybe he was just tired of the fussing and fighting inside the house and didn't want more of it outside.

My home life was not perfect, but it was close to it. Neither Mom nor Dad drank alcohol of any description. Dad did not smoke or buy pornographic magazines. Even though Mom had been poor as a child, she was comfortable living with Dad, a computer operator at Ford Motor Company. It was not a high paying job, but a good job with decent benefits. They argued some, but not often, and not usually in our presence. We were a Christian family. Dad was the head of the family and made the tough decisions. He loved Mom dearly, and together they loved us dearly, making sure we had a good childhood. When I went out to play, it was without the emotional baggage that my cousins were accumulating and lugging around with them, so I maintained that innocent view on life a lot longer than they did.

The summer of 1968 began for the boys of Enon Road with school letting out right before Memorial Day. The great news was that we had all passed. In the fall of that year, I was being promoted to the seventh grade. Cliftondale Elementary had 1st through 7th grades, so I would be in my "senior" year there. All the other cousins passed, too, except for Stevie, who was not able to go to school due to his emotional disability. No one understood it, and doctors could not explain it, but Stevie could not control his anger or other emotions. Often, in our ballgames, he would storm off the field over the littlest incident, and he usually was in his own imaginary world in the outfield. We had to constantly holler at him to be alert, and sometimes being ripped back to reality would set him off. He was a good kid and never hurt anyone, but he would scream, cry, and lose total control over what the rest of us considered the most normal and insignificant event or detail. It was impossible, of course, even with medication for him to function in a school setting, so what schooling he got, he got at home. That summer his mother, Aunt Vivian, hired me to come over to help teach Stevie how to read. Often if he could not grasp a concept or spell a word correctly as we sat there at the dining room table, he would run from the room, screaming. I would wait for him to come back, and if he did not or came back still upset, then I would pack up and go home. It was frustratingly slow for both of us. I had never taught anyone to read, and he was very impatient in wanting to learn to read. In the end he could read frontward, backward, sideways, and upside down. I didn't teach him that. I think I just pushed him along the way, and he learned everything else on his own. Stevie may have been different and may have been in his own little world much of the time. It was mostly a sports world where he was announcing games only he could see, but Stevie was no fool. He learned to use his problem to manipulate people and to get his way. He remembered everything he learned, even detailed facts like every vital statistic of every ballplayer in every sport. Stevie knew it, and he could discuss any sport or politics in depth with anyone who took the time to listen. Stevie was part of our gang, but that was mostly for the ballgames. He had little interest in our war games in the woods, fishing, or biking. He loved to play ball, but that, too, could be frustrating, especially if he was called out. When trying to beat out a throw to first base, if he was out, he just kept running and screaming, then dashed inside in tears. Sometimes his brother, Little Dickie, would hold the game up to go and try to calm Stevie down and get him back in the game. Sometimes we would let him be safe just to keep him happy and playing. On a good day, when his medication had him under control and Stevie had himself under control, he was as humorous and fine a companion as you could want to be around.

CHAPTER THREE

≫ *School Is Out* ≪

S chool was out. We would not even think about school again until blue jean buying time, school supply buying time, and church revival time in August. We always bought our school clothes right before school was to start again. Homecoming and revival came during the second week of August, which signaled the unofficial end of our summer vacation. That was months in the future, however, and on the first Monday out of school, we all slept late. At 9:00 am I was finally up. I had a leisure breakfast of Cheerios while watching a Roger Ramjet cartoon, and then pedaled off on my bike to see if any of the cousins were outside yet.

We lived in our own little conclave; our own family group of homes. Despite being so close to Atlanta, we were comfortably out in the country, where Grandpa and his brother Johnny had purchased 125 acres on both sides of Enon Road. It included a perfect sight for a pond; a small, run down sharecropper's house across the street that they rented out to poor families; a nice barn; and lots of pasture land for the cattle they raised. Grandpa's house was in the middle of our complex, sitting about 100 yards off the road. To his left was his brother, my great-uncle, Johnny. His wife, my great aunt Alma, was generous. She paid us exorbitant amounts to cut her yard in the sum-

mer time and to rake her leaves and clean her gutters in
the fall. To the right of Grandpa's house was the small
house that my Uncle Gene and his family lived in. Both
Gene and Lois worked, but that tiny house was still all
they could afford. They just couldn't seem to manage the
money they made. We lived beside Uncle Gene in a small,
red brick house on the two acres of land that my grand-
father gave to Mom as a wedding present. Across the
street lived one poor family after another, moving in and
out as rent came due that couldn't be paid, even as low as
the rent was. When one of the tenant's daughters killed
herself in that house, Grandpa quit renting it. Years later
when my wife was "expecting" our first child, we tore the
house down under orders from the county. We filled the
deep well there full of rocks from the house's foundation.
In front of Grandpa's house—between his house and the
road—was a large yard with a line of small pecan trees
that served as a boundary line for football games in the
fall and winter. The trees bore little fruit and did nothing
but get in the way during baseball season. Aunt Vivian
and her family had moved in with Grandma and Grandpa
when moving back from a job transfer from Chicago,
and they just stayed. When Grandpa retired a few years
later and he and Grandma moved to Florida, Aunt Vivian inherited the house. It was a large, two-story frame
house with a small front porch, a cement driveway, and
with huge oak trees in the backyard. When the Cuban
Missile Crisis hit in the early Sixties, Grandpa built a fall-
out shelter between his house and ours. The shelter was an
underground, basement-type room surrounded by cement
and lots of steel. It was supplied with United States Army
surplus cots, mattresses, and canned food. We had a path

up the hill from our yard, past Uncle Gene's front door, up to Grandpa's backyard. Our usual routine was to ride our bikes up our driveway, down the road to Grandpa's driveway, and then down the path back home.

Some days we spent hours and hours just riding our bikes along that path, or maybe just up the cement driveway and around Grandpa's house, time and time again. We kept a careful eye on our speedometers to see how fast we were going or how far we had been. Of course, we attached baseball cards to the spokes with clothes pins. This would make a loud flapping noise when rolling that the kids loved, but it irritated the adults, which is why we did it. On this first day out of school, I was working on my third mile up and down and around the house when the first cousin finally appeared around 10:15 am. He was still in his pajamas, hair sticking wildly in every direction, sleep cementing his eyes together as he tried to focus in the bright sunlight. It was Little Dickie. I stopped my bike in front of the steps where he was standing.

"Can you come out?" I asked. He rubbed his eyes lazily.

"I am out," he yawned. "Can't you see?"

That retort did not sit well with me, but I chose to ignore it. I wanted companionship too badly. "I mean can you come out and do something?"

He yawned again, scratched himself, and continued rubbing his eyes. "And do what?"

I pushed up on my bike seat, seeking a more comfortable spot. "Anything. Want to go fishing? I can go dig some worms while you're getting ready."

"Nah," he said. "I can't go fishing. Cartoons will be on in a minute."

"How about some baseball, then?" I asked hopefully.

"Later."

"How much later?" I was skeptical now that "Richard" would ever get out of his pajamas on this day.

"Just later."

I pushed up on the pedals and rode off, leaving Dickie to gaze after me. By the time I had made the turn at the head of the driveway, he had gone back inside. I rode another couple of laps, then on a sudden whim, I veered off onto the dirt road to the lake. It was nothing more than an old logging trail, barely passable to trucks in good weather. It was all down hill, though, and was a perfect ride for a bike with plenty of jumps, turns, and a downhill straight that concluded after a half mile. I pedaled by the barn. It was now a storage place for old, unwanted and unneeded family furniture. I glided into the tree shaded part of the road that ran past a garbage dump of sorts for the worn out family appliances and other trash. That carried me past the black walnut tree, now with a few little green nuts beginning to grow in clusters, and past the mock orange or Osage orange tree. Around a curve, the descent to the lake began. I finally cruised into an open area in front of the green, rippling water where trucks could park—if they could get there—or tents could be set up for campouts. I didn't bother to use my kickstand but let the bike drop. The boat was there, a 16 footer. It was aluminum and was always turned over with its back shining to the sky so it would not fill up with rainwater. I grabbed a grasshopper I saw on a blade of grass, and stepping quickly down to the brackish water's edge, threw it in. Within seconds there were swirls around it as it kicked vainly to reach shore. Suddenly, "swoosh," and it was gone as a large bream inhaled it. I caught two or three more grasshoppers and was fascinated each time as the fish would suck them down. From the far side of the lake I heard a tremendous splash. Though it was too far away to see the rings circling out from the area, I knew a large bass had come up from the depths to feast on a frog. The blood began racing through my veins. There was only one fish in that pond large enough to make a splash that could be heard all the way across the lake. It had to be "The Grandpa," "The Lake Leviathan," "Moby Bass."

The dream of all the boys of Enon Road was to hook "The Grandpa," the fish of legend that my dad had hooked one time and fought for an hour before losing him. World record! It just had to be a world record. Now, hearing the splash, my pulse quickened as I envisioned myself catching the great one. Hurriedly, I pushed my bike back up the hill and rode quickly home. I dashed to my room and snatched my fishing gear, my shotgun, and the boat paddle from their place in the corner. The lust for "The Fish" was upon me. Before noon, in the real heat of the day, I was in the boat and paddling across the water to the home of "Moby Bass." I silently approached the cattails on the dam, near the deepest part of the lake where we all knew this fish lived. I couldn't wait to get my plastic worm, a black flip-tail like my dad had used when he hooked him, into the water. As soon as I was twenty-five yards from the spot, I laid the paddle down and waited with my rod and reel as the boat glided into position. There was no wind and no drift, so the boat slowly stopped. Instantly I let fly with a cast, which landed just inches from the cattails. Amazed, I watched the line begin to glide immediately out towards deep water. Bass on! I felt the line between my thumb and index finger. It was moving. I let the fish run long enough to get the hook firmly in its mouth and then reeled slowly up until I felt the line tighten. Bam! I jerked back on the rod with all my weight and felt the hook sink into fish jaw. The fight had begun, and already the fish was coming to the surface to break water. And there it was, all ¾ pounds of fighting mad yearling bass. Its tail danced on the water before splashing loudly back into the lake with a resounding smack. I reeled it in, happy to catch a fish, but disappointed in the size and that it wasn't "The Bass." Our conservative estimate, not having ever seen it, put the giant fish at twenty-five pounds. The size of this little fish reminded me of the first bass I had caught in that lake not too many years before. I had proudly run with it up to the house and showed Grandpa. Grandpa was not a large man, and though his hair was silver gray, he had a head full of it that contrasted with his dark skin. Grandpa loved his grandkids. He laughed and giggled when he saw how excited I was about that little fish. Before too many minutes had elapsed, he was driving me back down to the lake in his 1959 green Chevrolet Apache pickup. To my amazement and everlasting joy, he took me out in the boat and showed me all his favorite spots, and he let me fish each with two or three casts. It was a great afternoon, just a boy and his grandpa, the boy having the time of his life in moments he would remember and cherish forever.

I turned this little bass loose. It was so small that it would be food for the legendary monster I was after. As I sat there, I noticed how close to the shore the boat had drifted. I paddled back out to the middle of the lake and made a few more casts. It was blistering hot, so I took off my shirt to get my first real sunburn of the year. I could hear the crows in the distance chasing off a red-tailed hawk, and I saw a few turtles stick their heads slowly and suspiciously out of the water before diving quickly back under. Rowing down to the shallow end of the lake, I fished among the submerged logs, stumps, and other natural trash on the lake bottom without getting another strike. I loved it there. It was just me, nature, the bass, the lake, the snakes, the turtles, and God, I supposed. Maybe someday I would be good enough, pray long enough, or work hard enough so that God would make that fish get on my hook. It wasn't this day, however, or on many days and nights of fishing in the future that the giant fish would be caught.

CHAPTER FOUR

⮞ *A Disappointing Afternoon* ⮜

Having missed lunch, my stomach was beginning to let me know that it needed food. Also, not having brought any water, and rowing and fishing being strenuous work at times, I was thirsty. I decided to go home. With any luck, Little Dickie would be out of his pajamas by now. After lunch we might get a ballgame up, go riding bikes, or go exploring in the woods. I paddled the boat to shore, unpacked it, pulled it up on the bank, and turned it over. It was a long walk home, carrying all the equipment, so it was nice when I walked in the door and Mom was there to offer me a glass of iced tea and ask me if I wanted any lunch. The great thing about tea in our house was that the sugar was put in while the tea was still hot. It came to the table extra sweet, which is how tea should be. Why folks haven't learned that you can't really sweeten cold tea, I will never know. The tea Mom made was good enough to be bottled and sold.

Within minutes of washing my hands and face, I was sitting in the kitchen. The fan was blowing across my quickly cooling brow, a sweating glass of tea at my right hand along with a cold meatloaf sandwich. It was lightly covered with mustard and ketchup, cut "cattycornered" just like I loved my sandwiches, and placed lovingly on my plate. Mom sat there with me, as she had already eaten, and we talked about fishing. She told me about the times she had caught fish in the lake years before. I think that somewhere in my deep subconscious, the Oedipus complex was being forged. Years later, I fell in love with a girl that could fish almost as good as I could. So we sat and talked. When I had finished, she went outside to get the wash off the clothesline. The clothes dryer had not yet made its appearance on Enon Road. She brought the basket of clothes in as I was nibbling on a cookie, but she did not ask me to help her fold the clothes. She had learned a long time before that folding clothes was something that little boys were just not adept at doing. At least her little boys weren't. I had heard stories about how well my cousins could do it, but I refused to believe anything like that.

Finishing and savoring that lunch, I noticed that Mom had now moved from the clothesbasket to the sink and was washing dishes. Mom washed a lot of dishes with three boys, Dad, and herself in the house. That summer it seemed like her hands stayed red and slightly swollen from being in the water so much and from the detergent on her hands. Many times I would notice her wedding ring on the counter above the sink, put there when her fingers began to swell. Mom never complained. She just picked up a pair of rubber gloves at the store and used them until the latest episode of "dishpan hands" subsided. I had always imagined that a mother's hands should be soft, slightly plump, and smooth with beautifully manicured nails. But Mom's hands always seemed a little red, thin, bony, and rough. Those were the hands of a real mother.

Grabbing my ball glove after savoring my last swallow of cold tea, I pushed open the back door and rejoiced in the noise of it slamming behind me with Mom's almost concurrent cry, "Don't slam the door." Boys love to slam back doors almost as much as mothers hate to hear them. Our screen door was a constant odd job on Dad's "to do" list. We were constantly kicking the screen out at the bottom, letting in bugs or flies. Often when we went to push the door open, we missed the wood and hit the wire, pushing it out from the frame. Dad tried various braces or screen guards, and I don't know that anything ever really stood up to the test of three boys pouring in and out of that door at what Mom called "break neck" speed. But Dad tried valiantly, and we actually tried to do our best not to tear it up, though we practiced and prided ourselves on our slamming.

I put my ball glove on my bike handlebars and pedaled up the driveway. Then I went down the road, swung into Grandpa's driveway, and pulled quickly up the rocky part to the paved area. I sped around the house twice, back up to the rose bush, around it, then back to Grandpa's back door. There was Little Dickie, now wearing a ridiculous pair of plaid short pants with matching socks. He regarded me with boredom. His hair was combed with 10W40 motor oil, I thought, and plastered to his head. He wore a tight, pullover shirt with Mickey Mouse ears on the pocket. He also wore his Sunday shoes, so I knew there would be no baseball on this first summer holiday.

I pulled my bike up to Dickie's feet as he stood on the top step. "What's up, Dick?" I asked? "Goin' somewhere?"

"What makes you think that?" he asked, almost belligerently.

I wanted to be very careful, not wanting to start a

37

fight on the first day of summer. "Well, you look all dressed up. And you got your Sunday shoes on."

"Mom is taking us up to the matinee to see a movie. It's got space invaders in it." Dickie was excited, as anything to do with space aliens was his specialty. Many times he would actually miss a baseball game to watch a television program with some kind of corny spacemen in it. Dickie watched a lot of television. In my earlier days, television actually signed off at night and back on in the morning. Dickie often bragged that he would see both in a single day. I stayed up one night just to see the sign off. I saw the flag waving, heard the national anthem and saw jets racing across the television screen. Immediately after that, a test pattern came on with a terrible, high pitch wailing. It was the same in the early morning for sign on. Now, television runs 24 hours a day with no signing on and signing off and no test patterns. There is just a constant patter of infomercials, commercials, and news. If you want to buy a ladder, exercise bike, or "male enhancer," just stay up after midnight and you will find them all advertised. We had three basic stations that we could watch until Ted Turner came along and started up his empire. Now with all the other channels and programming available, there is just more of nothing to watch. In those days, we didn't want to get caught watching the after lunch soap operas. We lived for Saturday morning, which was all cartoons on all channels until noon, unless we got reruns of "Sky King" or "Fury" or "My Friend, Flicka." I am convinced that access to 24 hours of television would have killed Dickie. He loved anything to do with space, all cartoons, and even considered himself an expert on dinosaurs. Once he tried to tell us that Dino, the Flintstone's dinosaur, was not really a dinosaur at all. We knew Dino was no T-Rex, but he was a dinosaur of some sort.

I heard the door open, and out came Little Dickie's brothers. His youngest, fair haired and skinned Jimmy, and Stevie, who would be my student starting the next Monday, hurried down the steps. Stevie was already in his own little world, and Aunt Vivian had to call to him as he wandered off around the house. "Stevie, get in the car."

Aunt Vivian was Mom's younger sister, and they dearly loved each other. Both were extremely proud of their boys. I didn't understand what a test living with Stevie could be until I began teaching him to read. Now I wonder if that put a strain on my aunt's and uncle's relationship, also. Vivian tended to try to pacify Stevie and to give in to his every whim, just to keep him from screaming. Uncle Richard would warn Stevie, as he did his other sons, before spanking them: "One. . . . .Two. . . . .Three." If he got to three and they weren't finished doing whatever it was they weren't supposed to be doing, then they got their "whoopin." To most kids it was a whipping, but when Uncle Richard got his belt out, even if it was only two licks, it was a "whoopin." Stevie would often just scream the louder and dash off into the woods or into the house to hide in his room when his Dad got to "One." Stevie could not stand any kind of pressure, especially of a competitive nature. Anytime he failed at anything, he would go off on his "tizzy," as Grandma called it. The kids were especially good at cajoling, begging, and apologizing to Stevie because we often needed his body on the field as a player. While he was not the best of athletes, he could chase a ball, and he could hit it once in a while.

I think Stevie had learned that he could manipulate

us with his "fits" because Stevie was very shrewd. Often, I thought that his emotional distresses came because he was so very smart and had just crossed the line on the upper end of the scale. I lost all doubt as to Stevie's intelligence when I began to teach him to read, and he learned so fast.

Aunt Vivian, to be polite, asked me if I wanted to go with them, but I noted the annoyed look on Dickie's face. Not wanting anything to do with watching a goofy movie on space invaders when there was so much to do outside, I quickly and gracefully declined.

Watching them drive away, I breathed a sigh of relief and once again pedaled for home.

Summer was not starting out like I had imagined it might. There would be no baseball game that day, but if everything went well, we could have the opening game of the "plastic bat and ball season" after supper. Grandpa might even make an appearance on the porch to cheer us on and to referee any disputes.

I was to be disappointed again. Stevie had "shown out" at the afternoon matinee, erupting into a terrible fit right there at Greenbriar Mall while standing in line for their movie tickets. Dickie claimed that Jimmy started it, and Jimmy claimed that Stevie started it. Stevie was too upset for days to even talk about it. Dickie later confided in me that he had started a game of tapping Stevie on the shoulder from behind so that Stevie would not know who did it. After the third tap, Stevie scowled. Turning quickly, Stevie caught Jimmy about to tap him. There was a push, then Jimmy pushed back, and Stevie fell. He scrambled up and ran away screaming into the crowd of kids and mothers gathered to watch the movie. Vivian had given

Dickie and Jimmy a terrible look and started in pursuit. Two minutes later, she found Stevie struggling between two security guards at the entrance to Rich's Department Store where he had tried to dive into the fountain. She quickly explained, but she still had to get the other two boys and leave the mall. Aunt Vivian was completely embarrassed, frustrated, and upset. Not knowing what else to do, she sentenced Jimmy and Dickie to a week of in house suspension, which to us was the equivalent of doing twenty years in a real prison. Stevie was gently warned by his mother and was promised a "whoopin" by his dad, which sent him off again. Both Grandma and Grandpa just shook their heads at him when they heard about the disturbance. The positive thing for me was that there would be no more trips to the mall for the afternoon matinee during that summer. We did not have the ballgame that night, but I knew that adult punishments never went the distance. Sure enough, by the next afternoon, we were playing baseball in the front yard.

CHAPTER FIVE

➤ *Lightning Strike?* ➤

"Fire!" My younger brother Andy and cousin Brad came boiling up out of the woods with the word "fire" bellowing out of their lungs with every step. Both, at age eleven, could be heard all over the neighborhood. Andy had soot marks across his cheeks, and it looked like Brad's eyebrows were singed. This was evidence of their first having tried to fight the fire before running for help. I was in the front yard, kicking up grasshoppers for a fishing trip, when I heard them. Mom, whose "Mommy Radar" was always on, came busting out of the screen door (tearing out Dad's most recent repair in the process). Hearing the yelling, she thought the house was on fire. "Fire!" Andy roared as he reached the carport. "All the woods are on fire!"

I looked towards the woods where they were pointing and saw the first plumes of smoke starting to rise into the sky just above the trees. I knew that it was near our trail that led to the lake road. As dry as it had been, it could quickly become a serious situation. Grabbing a rake that was leaning against the house, I ran for the woods. Uncle Gene, who was recovering from hernia surgery, heard the commotion from the porch of his house. He was already gently hobbling in that direction. Running as fast as I could with the rake in my hands, I followed my nose and soon found a fire line. It was about 50 yards long, burning towards the houses along the ground, but fortunately not up in the trees. Blue and gray smoke was thick in the air, which I could taste on my tongue and feel in my watering eyes. Within a minute, Andy and Brad ran up behind me. Each had a jug of water, which they began to pour on the fire. It was comical, and I had to laugh, because it would have taken literally thousands of jugs of water that size to put out that fire. Not knowing what to do, over the cackle and pop of the burning brush, I hollered, "How did it start?"

Brad looked at Andy, the older of the two by several months. Andy yelled back, "I don't know. We just came walking by and it was burning. Must have been lightning or something." I knew that was a story he had concocted on the spot, but the truth would have to wait. At the moment, the wind was blowing the smoke into our faces, and the fire was burning closer. We were the only thing between the fire and our houses. By this time, Uncle Gene arrived on the scene with his middle son, Larry, and began to mobilize our fire fighting force.

"Quick," he hollered, in pain from where his surgery had not altogether healed. "Break off some pine tops and start beating it."

He showed us how, and soon the five of us had green pine tops thrashing all up and down the fire line. Uncle Gene worked with a handkerchief tied on his face. His right hand was on the pine top, and his left hand held his surgical wound. The rest of us were beating and whipping those pine treetops into the fire for all we were worth to smash the fire out. Often one of us would look up to find our pine top on fire. We would throw it back into the fire before running to break off another one. Smoke continued to billow up from the burning pine straw and from the underbrush as the fire licked its way towards us. It wasn't long before Little Dickie arrived with Stevie and Jimmy, their mother having received a frantic call from my mother. Little Dickie and Jimmy each broke off pine tree limbs and joined us in the battle against the flames, slapping and flapping against the fire and the smoke. Uncle Gene looked up to encourage Stevie to do the same. When Stevie saw Gene's face, soot covering the white handkerchief that was still wrapped around his nose, Stevie turned and raced hysterically back towards the house in terror. He gave our mothers, who were waiting anxiously on our porch, a terrible report. He said that we were surrounded, trapped by a raging wall of fire, and that we were dying. He claimed Uncle Gene's face was burned off and that all was certainly lost. Tears were streaming down his face. He was trembling and almost fainted. Hearing his report, Mom finally sprang into action, fearing the situation was out of control. Pulling two blankets off the clothes line, she sped around behind the house and soaked them with the water hose. She lugged the dripping blankets back around the house to where her sister, Vivian, stood with Stevie under her arm. "Here," Mom said as she handed her a wet blanket. "Let's go get our boys."

Leaving Stevie collapsed on the porch, both women ran as fast as they could into the woods with the heavy blankets to where the fire was still raging out of control. Even though they were much relieved to see that no one had been hurt and that Gene's face had not been burned off, they knew the danger of the situation. Immediately, they began beating the burning straw with their wet blankets. With that help, the fire was finally brought under control after about ten more minutes of vicious stomping, whomping, blanket flapping, and pine top thrashing. Poor Uncle Gene was exhausted. He was hunched over in pain, holding himself oddly, and moaning. Leaving the boys to keep their eye on the smoldering ashes in case it flared back up, Mom and Vivian got on either side of their brother and escorted him gently back home, where he spent the rest of the day in agony. A trip to the doctor proved he had done nothing more than pop a stitch or two and tear some muscles. As they walked off, Aunt Vivian turned her head and called to Little Dickie. "Bring one of those hot pine tops with you when you come. I'm going to wear that Stevie out for scaring us to death." In the days following "The Great Fire," whenever Stevie started to get out of control around Aunt Vivian, all she had to say was, "Go get me that pine top." Stevie would get this look of fear in his eyes, but he would control himself.

In the meantime, the fire brigade just sort of stood around, beating a hot spot here and a hot spot there for fun. Andy and Brad looked much relieved, while Little Dickie was already telling how he had saved Uncle Gene several times in the firefight. I knew that by the end of the day, he would have convinced himself that he had single handedly put out the fire that was about to consume us and our houses. I found the rake I had laid down and began raking a fire breakaway from the burned area. Looking back to Andy, I said, "There wasn't any lightning today."

He just looked at me. "Then I guess somebody must have thrown down a cigarette or something."

"Yeah," I said, "or something." He did not reply. It was not until years later that he and Brad finally told the truth of playing with matches and starting the fire that quickly got out of hand. Grandpa got home from work that afternoon and heard the story from Little Dickie about how he had rescued Gene. He heard another version from Jimmy, an emotional wailing version of it from Stevie, and a coherent version from Vivian. When he walked down to see it, he got another version from me, Andy, and Brad. Grandpa knew what had happened; he was nobody's fool. But no one was hurt, and no real damage was done. It was a hard lesson that Brad and Andy learned. Grandpa knew that none of us would ever play with matches or start fires in those woods again. It may have been the activities of that day that led to my life long ambition to be a "Smoke-Jumper,"—a forest fire fighter who jumps in and fights the fire on the ground while airplanes drop chemicals on it from above. I never realized that dream, but there was that one day in my life when I had been a real forest fire fighter.

CHAPTER SIX

➣ *Downtown* ⋖

There were many days when I thought that we lived in a netherworld, an existence not in the city, yet not really in the country. We were only fifteen minutes from a mall, which had a J.C. Penny's where we got our blue jeans for school. It also had a Woolworth's with a great restaurant in it that served the best, greasiest hamburgers anywhere. There was a twin theatre; a Rich's Department store, which had an elegant "Magnolia Room" upstairs (I never entered it in my life); a Chick-fil-a fast food place; and assorted little shops and stores up and down the mall. We couldn't really consider ourselves country. We lived with no neighbors except our relatives and were isolated between two main roads. Stonewall Tell Road was several miles to the right, or to the west, and Campbellton Road was many more miles to the left, or to the east. Campbellton Road ran through Ben Hill to the new mall. Until the mall came, we would go downtown to the Rich's Bargain Basement to buy our school clothes. I remember walking along the downtown Atlanta streets with the skyscrapers looming over us; with the scary beggars sitting along the walls selling pencils; and with the wonderful window full of cakes from the Rich's Bakery. Buses would roar by with their diesel fumes puffing out behind them, while cars would honk and people would scurry across the streets of traffic. I was always glad to get home from the city. That was one time when I was not ashamed to hold my mom's hand in public as she pulled us along after her.

I often wished on these trips that old Will Hawkins, who lived across the street from us for a while in the rental house, could have gone with us. The legend was that he once walked to Ben Hill to catch the bus into Atlanta, carrying his shotgun the whole way. I would have felt a lot safer with grizzled Will Hawkins stalking beside me through the downtown streets. There is something about a man with a shotgun that most folks, even beggars, just will not bother.

The trip to the city was always an experience for us. It was a chore for Mom and Dad, unless we were going downtown at Christmas time to ride the Pink Pig at Rich's Department Store. The Pink Pig was the wonderful ride that circled above on the store ceiling as people shopped below. If you were a child near Atlanta, you rode the Pink Pig at some point in your life. That was as much of a ritual as sitting in Santa's lap. At Christmas, Rich's had the unique ride glide along on tracks attached to the ceiling as it carried kids and parents alike high above toy land and Santa Claus.

Back at the safety of home on Enon Road, there was no traffic on the tar and gravel road, which would ooze the black stuff on hot, summer afternoons. If you walked on it at all, the tar would get on your shoes. You would track it inside, and Mom would howl. Enon Road ran between Stonewall Tell and Campbellton Road. In 1968, we were the only ones living there in our own little settlement in that wilderness. We were the first pioneers in an area that would eventually boast of subdivisions, a high school, and an Olympic shooting venue that opened Enon Road to the world. As you rode down Enon, you would see open pasture land that was cut through by Camp Creek. You would also see miles and miles of nothing but hardwoods and pines. Our homes were in an opening in that forest at the confluence of Miles and Enon Road. You could drive up Grandpa's driveway and go straight across Enon directly onto Miles. Miles was an uphill pull on a bike, so we seldom ventured up either walking or riding our bikes, though the ride back down was worth the work to get up it. There were a few more people living on Miles, but there were no kids to play with, no ball fields, and no stores. We had little reason to go that way unless we riding with our folks to church.

We were far enough out in the country that we ran out in the yard and gawked anytime a helicopter came over. We had long before adjusted to the airplane noise from Atlanta Airport, but there was just something about the throbbing and drumming of any passing helicopter that we could not resist. Once in a long while, a column of army copters would pass over, row upon row, copter upon copter. We would stand amazed, gazing into the sky until our necks ached and the last one had passed over, its rumbling engine finally dying away in the distance.

We saw few cars during the day on Enon Road, except for the mailman around noon and the paper man around suppertime. There were the other occasional delivery people, but that was about all the traffic we saw on the road. We never saw a police car, fire truck, ambulance, or big 18-wheeler. We were isolated, yet close enough to stores, theaters, small towns, and big cities that we had the best of all possible worlds. Fortunately we were close enough to the volunteer fire department that they were able to save Dad's workshop one night when it really was hit by lightning.

CHAPTER SEVEN

⇒ *Dogs* ⇐

D ogs played a big part in our lives. The only cat I can remember ever having was a big, yellow tomcat that we called "Boots," of course. I remember watching him be born at the minute that Alan Shepherd was rocketing into space for his first, short ride. Boots died at a ripe old age many years later, laying his tired body down right in front of the door so that we would be sure not to miss him. We were really dog people. Through the years we had an assortment of dogs—mongrel yard dogs mostly—whose moms were neighbors' dogs and whose daddies had just been passing through. We were into show dogs for awhile. We raised Cairn Terriers, which dad called "bouncies" because of their ability to bounce all over the yard. Mom and Dad spent several hundred dollars on a pedigreed female whom we called "Lady." Mom showed her a time or two at local kennel club shows. She quickly found out that it mattered less how good the dog was and more who you really were, how much money you had, and how well connected you were at the kennel club, which we were not. Years later, when Lady was old, tired, gray, arthritic, and in a lot of pain, Dad asked me to take the .22 rifle and put her out of her misery, which I did. I felt bad about that afterwards, but that was how things were done on Enon Road in 1968.

Tiger was our yard dog that summer, a mix between

a Manchester terrier and some other mixed breed. He looked like a Chihuahua on steroids because he was muscular and carried himself like you had better not get in his way. He was brown, had straight ears, the typical short legs, shorthair, and the highest vertical leap of any dog living in 1968. Grandpa would often take us down to the lake in his deep green Chevrolet Apache truck. We loved riding in the back, especially when going through the woods where the limbs would slap at us. Tiger loved to ride, too, and we were always letting him jump up on the lowered tailgate to go with us. One day, however, Tiger was nowhere to be seen as we piled into the truck for a trip around the pasture, so we did not bother putting the tailgate down. When Grandpa cranked that truck up, Tiger must have heard it. We had just started moving forward when Tiger came charging up the hill as fast as his little dog legs could carry him. Never slowing down, he leaped forward and sailed over the raised tailgate right into the back of the truck amongst all the boys who were hollering, laughing, pushing, squirming, and rolling around. That was a mighty leap for a little dog with stubby legs. Fortunately, there were plenty of our bodies back there to slow his forward motion. Without us, he would have slid right into the back wall of the truck, no doubt flattening himself so badly that folks would have thought he was a Pug.

Little Dickie's dog was a proud looking dog, a pure bred Cocker Spaniel. His name was Colonel. If there ever was a dog that had no common sense but loved to run, rip, and nip at the kids' heels, it was Colonel. The dog would also stand in one spot and bark for hours and hours for no apparent reason. We figured he was so dumb that he barked at tree leaves when the wind blew, or at pine-cones when they fell off of the trees. We suspected that many times he was barking at his own shadow. The dog was dumb. He would not ride in the truck. If forcibly put there, he would wrestle and fight until turned loose so he could jump out. I guess he figured that if God had meant him to travel that way, he would have put tires where his paws were. Little Dickie loved Colonel. He always threw it in our faces that his dog had a pedigree. Colonel's father was a show dog, and his mother was a champion. Little Dickie was always making fun of Tiger. He always wanted to see his pedigree and asked what Tiger's "Real AKC registered" name was. So naturally, we hated Colonel all the more. If ever Colonel showed up without Dickie, rocks and sticks were sure to fly his way. Sadly, late one Friday afternoon, the only vehicle on the road that day besides the mailman hit Colonel as he was returning home from some amorous adventure up on Miles Road. We attended Colonel's funeral the next morning. It was out behind Grandpa's house where Uncle Richard had dug a shallow grave. We boys joked that as flat as he was, it didn't need to be too deep. Colonel was buried with full military honors, including us boys whistling "Taps" for him at the end. Stevie did not attend. He had gone into hysterics at the news, but the rest of us were there to pay our respects. If we hated the dog, we certainly had not wanted him to be flattened by Mr. Powell's fully-loaded-with-concrete-blocks, one-ton Ford pickup. Little Dickie held his mom's hand as we stood by the grave. The stiff form of the dog wrapped in a blanket was gently lowered into the hole. As the first shovel of dirt went on, Dickie broke completely down. Tears streamed off his face like rain drops.

His mother quietly picked up her sobbing son and carried him to the house with little brother Jimmy following sadly. The rest of us stood around watching as Uncle Richard covered Colonel with dirt, and then we ran home to watch cartoons. We were amazed a week later when Little Dickie loudly proclaimed a new Cocker Spaniel puppy had been purchased and would soon take over as their new dog. He would be named "General." We all hoped that General would be smarter than his predecessor, but we did not hold out much hope.

CHAPTER EIGHT

⇒ *Dickie Drops the Ball* ⇐

The little white ball flew towards me through the gloom. With one hand on the bat, I swung as hard as I could. I was the last batter in our two-hour-long game of plastic bat and ball. We were behind 43–42. It was getting dark quickly, and in the distance I heard Mom calling us home for the third and final time. Dickie was pitching in relief of his brother Stevie, who had had an amazing game. He held us to only 42 runs, struck out 19, and hit three homeruns over the driveway, which was the plastic bat and ball homerun mark. Stevie had never played so well or so long without getting upset. I suspected he was on some new medication, that the moon phase was right, or that the vision of his dad sitting on the porch, watching with a pine top beside him, had kept him in line. But Stevie had played wonderfully and was about to win his first game ever as pitcher. He had wanted to pitch, but Dickie had been against it until his dad said to give him a chance. Stevie had struck me out three times. I had been swinging for the fences, but I had hit five homeruns off of him, too, the last four in a row. Dickie knew I had Stevie measured. The last inning started with Stevie still pitching, and he struck Andy out. Dickie was hollering encouragement from the outfield, where he stood behind the driveway. This was legal because as long as you caught the ball, it did not matter whether it was over the driveway or not.

Lightning bugs had started their nightly ascent from the grass and were already flashing in the air as Stevie pitched to Brad. Brad hit it long and far, but Dickie quickly ran up under it and caught it for out number two. In the distance, I heard Mom's first call to come home. Dark was falling fast. Stevie pitched, and I swatted a single right back through his legs. My younger brother, Andy, came up next and slashed a line drive past Jimmy, who was playing between first and second. I ended up on third base. Brad then hit a little pop over Stevie, who lost it in the porch lights—or so he said. It fell in for a hit. I scored, making it 43–42. It was my turn to bat. I heard Mom's second call to come home. In the silence that followed, I heard a whippoorwill in the distance. Chimney sweeps, or bats, were circling overhead, diving and ducking for their nightly feast of insects. Andy was now on third base, which was nothing more than the crack on the cement walk at the edge of the house. There was not a lot of foul territory in our little ball field in front of the house. Brad was on first, which was a small board flat on the ground to the side of a stickly bush that marked the first base foul line. It was getting darker, but Dickie still trotted slowly in from the outfield to talk with Stevie. Dickie had a flair for the dramatic. Jimmy came in for the huddle, too, and they argued. Stevie was becoming visibly upset, but when he heard Uncle Richard flop the pine top on the cement porch where he was sitting, he slammed the ball into Dickie's hand and stormed into centerfield. Dickie would be pitching in relief to me.

Dickie always had a sense of heroics. He knew just when to insert himself into whatever event would bring him the most glory. He now had it figured that with the darkness coming on and with two outs, he could save Stevie's greatest game by striking me out with a couple of fast balls. The odds were in his favor, or he would never have chanced it. It also gave him a great opportunity to make me look bad and to beat me for once, which he was seldom able to do at anything. With Grandpa and his dad sitting on the porch, watching just feet away, it was now Dickie's moment to shine and no longer Stevie's. The spotlight had shifted. I stood there at home plate, waving the bat as Dickie looked in at me. It was so dark that I could not see much more than his white t-shirt and the ball in his hand. Dickie reached back and threw the ball for all he was worth. By the rules, fastballs were not allowed unless you chose to swing at them, which I did on this occasion; I missed. I heard Stevie roar approval from the outfield when Dickie yelled, "Strike one." Andy fussed at Dickie for throwing too fast, and Brad chimed in that Dickie was cheating. But Dickie, knowing the rule, quoted it as if it were really written down somewhere.

"I can throw as fast as I want as long as he swings."

The second pitch was fast, also, and up in my eyes. I never even saw it, but I swung crazily and missed again. "Strike two, strike two," Dickie called for everyone to hear. Stevie roared again. In the distance, I heard Mom's final call. This was it. Down to the last pitch; the last strike; the last out. Almost total darkness had enveloped the field. Dickie ground the ball wickedly on his hip—at least I thought I could see him doing that. Then Dickie threw the pitch that will be discussed even as we are carrying each other to the graveyard. For the rest of our lives, and into eternity if we have memories of earth there, we will talk about that pitch. Having thrown two "heaters" by me, Dickie knew I was ready for a third one and that I probably had him timed. Darkness or not, he didn't think he could get a third one by me. He wound up as if he was going to throw the fastest ball ever, as deception was part of his plan. He was going to throw a changeup, a pitch that you threw like it would be fast, but it would actually be slow. The hitter's timing would be off, so he would swing and miss. I was set up for it. But the changeup depends on deception and on the motion of the pitcher being the same with the fastball as the changeup. What Dickie did not realize was that I could not see his windup because it was so dark. All I could see was the whiteness of the ball. Instead of a speeding blur coming out of the dark—which I had no chance of hitting—I saw this slow moving, white ball floating to me, looking almost as big as a grapefruit. Dickie was always prone to extreme exaggeration, so he had exaggerated his windup, even throwing in a loud grunt for good measure. He threw the slowest pitch he could to fool me. With just one hand on the bat, I swung as hard as I could. The bat smacked the ball hard on the thickest part—plastic on plastic. The ball sailed away into the night. Long, far and high it flew, curving over the driveway as it disappeared into the gloom, chimney sweeps diving on it as it flew by. There was total silence for a brief moment. "Where did it go?" screamed Stevie, who had never seen it because he never even moved. All he had heard was the bat hitting the ball. Dickie was screaming, "Foul ball, foul ball." Jimmy, who had seen the ball fly off the bat, looked to the outfield, saying nothing. Andy raced in from third as I headed for first base in my homerun trot. I had not seen it, but as hard as I had hit it, I knew it was a homerun. Dickie stood screaming, "You can't run, it's foul." Stevie tore in from the outfield with, "Foul ball, foul ball," pouring out of him. I rounded second as Dickie and Stevie both swarmed around me, screaming that it was foul. Brad scored as they fussed, and I ran by them as they continued to holler. Jimmy just walked off the field with disgust, not even waiting to see what would happen next. I touched third as Dickie grabbed my shirt, but I pulled away and finally crossed home plate. Andy and Brad greeted me with slaps on my back. Stevie and Dickie appealed to the high court, to the supreme judge of judges, to the commissioner of all those plastic bat and ball games, Grandpa.

"I never saw it," he said. "Why don't you go and find the ball and see if it is in fair or foul territory? If it's in fair territory, it's a homer; if it's in foul, you finish the game tomorrow." That was the ruling, so we all went looking for the ball. Knowing that Dickie was not beyond finding it and throwing it into foul territory, I sent Andy and Brad to look with him. Before long, however, Grandma came out and said that Mom had called and we were to go home immediately. Aunt Vivian came out behind Grandma and called her boys in, too. We would have to wait until morning to find the ball.

I slept well that night but was up early. As soon as Dad left for work, Andy and I were running for the front yard. The grass was still wet with dew as we galloped across home plate and looked eagerly across the driveway into homerun territory for the ball. There were no footprints in the dew, so we knew we were the first ones there. We stopped on the driveway, looking this way and that for the ball. Hearing a door slam, we turned and saw Little Dickie come staggering out of the house. He was still in his Goofy pajamas, which were his favorites two years ago but now were much too small for him. The leg bottoms only reached his shins. His hair was wild, standing up in every different direction. Sleep still blurred his red eyes as he hopped gingerly towards us in his bare feet. He had not slept well. He had intended to be up at the first light of dawn to insure the ball was found in foul territory, but he had overslept. At least the search could be official without either side claiming the other had moved the ball. But we searched in vain. For over an hour we looked all over the outfield—in fair territory, in foul territory; in the bushes, under the bushes; under the car, on the roof—but the ball just was not there. We looked and looked. Brad and Jimmy came out and joined the search, but the ball was just not to be found. It never was found. Little Dickie was not amused when Brad said I must have hit that ball so hard and so high that it went into orbit. Then the argument began of what we should do next; whether we should play that last pitch over again, call the game a tie, or just forget about it. Andy and I finally went home to breakfast. As we left, we saw Dickie standing on the driveway, hands on hips, still perplexed as to where the ball had landed. After breakfast, we went back to the ball field. Dickie was still there in his pajamas but now had tennis shoes on without socks. He tried to begin the argument again.

"Look, Dickie," I said, cutting him off. "You know, I know, and everyone else knows that that ball was a home-run." Dickie tried to object, but I told him to shut up and listen. "Last night was the greatest game Stevie has ever played. Ever. He will never match it, and for it to end that way, well, it's just not right. I've had my great games, and so have you, but not him, and I say it's his turn. So here's the plan."

I reached into my back pocket and pulled another white, plastic ball that I had just brought from home. "You see this ball?" Dickie looked at it suspiciously. "No, it's not that ball. I just brought this one from home. I say that I go down to that tree in Aunt Alma's yard there in centerfield, pull down one of the limbs, and stick it in there. You know the rule. If a ball is caught coming off the house or out of a tree, it is still an out. So if the ball is in that tree, technically, the game is still going."

The light still had not gone off in Dickie's eyes. "So what good will that do?"

"I put the ball in the tree. We call Stevie, tell him we have found it, and that all you have to do is catch the ball before it hits the ground when we shake the limb, and you win."

Dickie looked from the tree to home plate and back to the tree. "Nobody ever hit one that far. Nobody could hit one that far, not even Uncle Gene. That would be the record. It could never be beat."

"You're right. I would get the record for the longest hit in plastic bat and ball history. Stevie gets the win, and you get the save. You beat us, we lose. Fair and square, no questions asked. Everybody gets something he wants."

Dickie mulled it over. Victory over me was a great enticement anytime. "OK," he said, "How do we work it?"

"I'll put this ball up in that low limb right there so that it will look like it landed there. You go in and get Stevie and Jimmy. Andy will run and get Brad. When we are all here, I will shake the limb and you catch it. That's all there is to it."

Dickie was still skeptical. "What if we don't catch it?"

"Oh, come on, Dickie," I replied, exasperated. "How could you not catch it?"

Dickie finally agreed, so he ran in hollering. He played his role perfectly, claiming that we had found the ball. Stevie came running out, still in his pajamas. Jimmy came in short pants and no shirt, and Brad arrived dressed for a trip to the dentist that he was about to make. All the boys gathered around in silent awe as they stared at the ball in the tree. It was a thing of legend; a Ruthian blow of fantastic proportion had put it there. As a breeze gently blew, Dickie quickly moved over just in case it fell. Stevie started to grab the ball in triumph, but I grabbed his arm and explained the rule. As long as the ball was in the tree, the game was not over. But he could not pick it from the limb. It had to be given a chance to fall.

"I'm going to shake the limb," I said. "Catch it and you win."

Stevie moved under the limb and joined Dickie. Jimmy moved in close. "Wait a minute," said Dickie suddenly. "Let me lay down under it, and if you miss it, I'll still catch it."

Dickie lied down on his back under the limb in the dew glistening grass, getting his favorite pajamas wet and stained. Even then, with the flair for the dramatic, the dream of being the hero welled up in him. When he was ready and Stevie and Jimmy were standing strategically hunched over ready for action, I gently grabbed the limb and pulled down. Then I let it flip up, hoping the ball would fly slowly up in the air where Stevie would catch it. It did fly up, maybe chest high, and it seemed to stop at its apex for an hour before it started its descent. I saw three hands grab for the ball simultaneously. Dickie sat up with a look of triumph on his face. He reached straight up rather than waiting for the ball to fall to him as planned. Stevie's hand and Jimmy's hand both seized at the ball at the exact same moment and place in space. I saw their hands and fingers jam against each other, and I heard the crack of knuckles and cries of pain and surprise. The ball fell past them and past Dickie's outstretched hand. It landed on his knees, rolled down his legs, and plopped gently onto the ground.

I picked the ball up in disgust. "Gosh, Dickie," I said. "You couldn't catch a cold."

With Jimmy and Stevie holding their swelling fingers as they moaned, Dickie squalled out the truth of my evil plan to steal Stevie's victory. He yelled that I had tricked him and lied to him. Andy, Brad and I walked back across the driveway and started for home. In the distance I could still hear Dickie crying out, "Foul ball. It was a foul ball!"

Meanwhile, at his electrical shop in East Point, Grandpa was giggling lightly. He was wondering what his grandsons were doing back home, but he had a good idea. He looked at the white, plastic ball on his desk and smiled.

CHAPTER NINE

⇒ *Death* ⇐

We didn't know much about death in that wonderful summer of 1968. Burying Colonel had been as close as we had come, and then we made jokes (not around the Duncans, of course) about him being flat as a pancake. We laughed and wondered if they had to scrape him off the tires and off the road. Then somebody got really gross and wondered if we went up to the spot in the road where he got killed if we might still find some of his guts laying around somewhere. Death was something to be laughed at and scorned and not taken seriously. The boys of Enon Road weren't sadistic and we didn't go around killing animals for no reason, but humor was the way we dealt with what little death we did face.

Ronnie arrived early in the summer of 1968. He was my Aunt Lois's half brother who had been kicked out of his home in south Georgia where Lois was raised. Lois, who loved everything and everybody—especially sixteen-year-old Ronnie—took him into her home, which was already overcrowded with three other growing sons. Ronnie was tall and had long hair that he constantly had to push out of his eyes. He was very quiet and had a strange look about him. I didn't know it then, but now that I have been out in the world and lived life and seen death, I know that look. It was the haunted look of death. It was the belief that the conscious mind does not acknowledge and will not admit, but the subconscious recognizes and shows it on the face . . . the belief that life hasn't been worth living. Life must be lived fast and hard because it won't last long, anyway. Ronnie had lived hard, and living with alcoholic Gene was not the influence he needed. Grandpa, who was always trying to give people a chance to do well, took Ronnie under his wing and let him work for him at Fulton County Electric that summer. Ronnie worked hard and did well. On the weekends, Ronnie would take time to play baseball with us. When he played, we had to turn our field lengthwise because he could hit the ball farther than all of us and we needed more outfield. We did not want him being the first to hit one over the road for a homerun.

Ronnie loved to fish. On one of our rare nighttime fish excursions, I invited Ronnie to fish in the boat with me, which he did. It was noisy on the lake in the summer, with all the frogs chattering, night birds screeching, and crickets chirping. Occasionally, fish slapped the water as they lunged skyward to grab a doomed frog or bug. I tried to strike up a conversation with Ronnie, but he just said, "You know, I think fishing is better when we are quiet." So I shut up and we fished in the dark, even more aware of the nightly noises around us. Throwing my plastic worm towards the shore, I judged the distance by looking at the lighter sky behind the darkened trees. We caught a few bass that night and went home after sunup—tired, but happy.

Uncle Gene had a little motor scooter that he had brought home for the kids, but it was worn out when he got it. He never could get it to work just right, so it was pushed out of sight behind the house. Ronnie saw it, and we found out he could have been a master mechanic. It wasn't long before he had that little scooter out and running. He could be seen zooming all over the yard with it. Because it was small and sat low to the ground, his butt hung over the seat. It was funny to see the blue smoke billowing out from the scooter when he was riding it.

But Ronnie had demons that possessed him. Being only twelve and naïve, I did not know it and could not see it. All we were told at the time was that he was spending the summer with Lois, but later I learned his step dad had beaten him often and hard. Ronnie had finally run away to find his sister, which he did. Even at sixteen, Ronnie had acquired a taste for alcohol. Often we would see him and Uncle Gene sitting on Gene's back porch and drinking a beer or two or three. Ronnie never shared his life with us. He never told us his last name, never told us what he wanted to do with life, and never told us where he was going to school in the fall, but we suspected nowhere. He would play ball if he was around and we were playing. He was always glad to fish with us if we didn't talk too much, and he loved working with Grandpa. He was a good guy, and we liked him a lot. Eventually he began to smile more than when he first arrived, and life seemed to be treating him right for once. Often my dad would invite him to come to church with us. Ronnie said he had never been to church and would not feel comfortable there since he did not have a suit, so he never went.

Ronnie finally did go to church two years later. He had gone back home to south Georgia at the end of that summer. He was out riding his motorcycle one night, drunk and without a helmet, when a logging truck pulled out in front of him. Poor Ronnie never saw the truck, so he never had a chance. When we heard the news, no one made jokes about scraping him up or about him being as flat as a pancake. Our age of innocence had ended by then, and death was something we had learned to dread. There wasn't much left of Ronnie to put into a casket. I heard later that they did have a nice funeral for him. Six of his drinking buddies carried his remains into the tiny community church—the first and last time he had ever gone to church. Yes, now I know the look I saw on Ronnie's face. It is the look that knows that life is short, so you had better live it hard and fast and cram all the living you can into it. Ronnie did, and that is what killed him—that and the alcohol that he got his hands on far too easily.

CHAPTER TEN

⇒ *Dickie Goes to a Camp Out* ⇐

It was about two weeks into our summer when Andy and Brad decided they wanted to go camping down at the lake with just them and some buddies. Mom and Aunt Lois reluctantly agreed. So on Friday afternoon Andy, Brad, and two of Andy's friends—Ben Turner and Foley Hendrick—piled all their camping gear into dad's tractor cart. I was given the assignment of driving them to the lake and helping them set up camp. Ben Turner was still mourning the loss of his mother earlier that year, so Mom thought it would be good to invite him. Foley was Andy's best friend. No one knew then that this tall, gangly, brilliant kid with the sunken chest would one day be Captain Foley Hendrick and would fly helicopters for the United States Army. With all the gear packed in the little cart and the boys walking behind, lugging what would not fit, I drove the little garden tractor down the washed out road to the lake. As instructed, I helped the boys set up camp. Before I left, I warned them to be careful of snakes, goblins, and "Old Rawhead and Bloody Bones," who would likely come out after dark. I left the tractor so they could load it for when I returned in the morning to drive them home.

Little Dickie had heard about the camp out. It was killing him that he had not been invited. So after his family finished supper, he came down to the house to see me.

As always, Dickie had a plan. We would wait until just about dark, then we would sneak down to the lake to spy on the boys. When it was real dark, we would run through their camp, screaming. It didn't sound like much fun to me, but I didn't have anything else to do. I grabbed a flashlight and told Mom I was going to check on the camp out. Dickie and I started through the gloom towards the lake. Even then Dickie had on short pants, black socks and Sunday dress shoes. It was not exactly what one should wear when traipsing through the woods at night, but then Dickie never did understand fashion. When we got to the hill above the lake, we saw the campfire crackling brightly, so we began to sneak quietly down to the edge of the trees. We sat there and listened, hearing the boys laughing and snickering in the tent. Andy was obviously telling dirty jokes since he was already wiser to the ways of the world than I was. And cussing! I heard several of the boys cuss, and they would laugh. Then one would say another word, and they would laugh some more. They were having a real good time being away from Mom and Dad. I suspected that cigarettes were being smoked, too.

Dickie was laughing so hard I thought he was going to give us away. He motioned for me to follow, and we snuck back up the trail. "I'm going to buzz the camp," he said. "I'll run through screaming, and you listen to what they do. It will be great!"

I should have stopped Dickie. But once Dickie got an idea, no matter how silly or crazy, there was no stopping him. He scurried through the night as I crouched in the bushes, watching. He ran up behind the tent and then he let out a blood curdling, terrible scream. He then dashed around the front of the tent, still screaming. Unfortunately,

Dickie did not see the rope that was strung from the top of the tent to a tent peg. He hit it and sprawled face first in the dirt. His motion yanked the rope free, which started the tent collapsing. With all the motion from inside as the boys tried to get out before they were murdered, the tent fell on the terrified campers as they struggled for the tent flap. I did not wait around. I left Dickie to his fate and ran back to the house.

About an hour later, I was sitting there watching television when Andy and his camp out crew came stumbling in, still quivering with fright and rage. Brad had been the first one out of the tent and had seen Dickie as he staggered off into the woods. Revenge was in their eyes, and divine retribution had already been devised many times on their long, terrifying walk in the dark to the house. My part in the little escapade was unknown to them until Mom heard the story. "I thought you went down to check on them," she said threateningly. "Did you do this?"

In all honesty, I confessed. "It was Little Dickie. He followed me down. Then he ambushed them."

Mom turned towards the telephone in the hall and said over her shoulder, "I will deal with you later, young man." I felt a sinking feeling in my chest as she stormed out. I had to face the silent stares of my brother and his friends.

I looked at them and simply said, "I heard everything y'all were saying."

"What do you mean 'everything'?" asked Andy cautiously.

"Everything," I answered, "that Mom wouldn't

want to know about. And by the way, who brought the cigarettes?"

It wasn't long before Mom came back with a smile on her face. It was some minutes before she could quit giggling long enough to tell us what had happened. "It seems that Little Dickie, in trying to escape from y'all after his 'raid,' couldn't find the road, got lost in the woods and ran into a briar patch." I knew the briar patch she was talking about. I knew it was wide and vicious. And suddenly I remembered Dickie's legs.

"But Mom," I said, slowly, "Dickie had on short pants."

Mom burst out laughing, as did Andy and his buddies. They laughed hard and long and actually had to wipe tears from their eyes. The picture of Dickie running blindly into that briar patch was too much for us.

When there was a break in their mirth, Mom giggled again. "I spoke to your Uncle Richard. He said that Aunt Vivian had Dickie in the bathroom putting Bactine and Mercurochrome on all the scratches." Mom paused for dramatic effect. "I could hear Dickie squalling in the background." Bactine and Mercurochrome, two medicines that were universally applied for any scratch or wound by moms all over America in 1968, stung worse than any other medicines ever invented by man. "And," Mom went on, "they are taking him to the doctor in the morning for a tetanus shot."

Mom then looked at me. "And what should we do with him?" Mom asked Andy and his friends, pointing to me. Andy looked me over with fear in his eyes.

"Nothing," he said. "He wasn't involved. Dickie did it, and he's been punished. Leave him alone."

Mom looked back and forth between us, wondering what had transpired while she was on the phone. "All right," she said, "if you say so. Now if you will excuse me, Vivian said Dickie's back is really scratched up, too. She needs me to bring up some Peroxide to pour on his back and arms." If Bactine and Mercurochrome were the two worst burning medications, then Peroxide was a close third. Poor Dickie.

CHAPTER ELEVEN

⇒ *The Bambino Strikes* ⇐

Summer was beginning to sizzle. Dickie was finally moving around again, showing off his scabs from the campout escapade. The boys of Enon Road once more were doing what they lived for in the summertime—playing baseball. This was baseball in its purest form; baseball as it was created to be; baseball without uniforms, umpires, or adult coaches. It was baseball with more strikes for the little guys, or letting the older boys take the third swing for the youngest kids. It was baseball with imaginary men running the bases when needed, or "ghost runners" as some city kids called them. It was baseball with arguments over whether you were safe or out, but arguing with each other and not some blind umpire. It was baseball without the frills; with only swinging strikes; with limited fair territory designed to match the number of players available to play that particular day. It was baseball with trees as outfielders at times, and baseball with the sticky tar road as the homerun mark. Not one of these boys of Enon Road in 1968 had yet hit one over, though they all expected it to happen any day; especially considering that I was the oldest and growing bigger and stronger every minute. I had hit several blasts to the edge of the road. One even bounced in the middle of the road for a ground rule double. The guys held their collective breaths just knowing that it was a homer. Hitting a ball over the road would be like beating Babe Ruth's homerun mark (as Henry Aaron was younger and still pursuing the Babe in those days). Hitting one over the road was the sacred mark; the goal that all the boys wanted to be the first to achieve; the Holy Grail of front yard baseball. The first one to do it would be immortalized in our minds forever.

Yes, this was baseball with old leather gloves handed down from older brothers or even dads. Several of the gang had newer, Christmas present versions with a professional ballplayer's name stenciled into the leather. This was baseball as it was played before the pampered, millionaire players got hold of it, and the businessmen agents and television revenue ruined it. This was baseball played for nothing but fun. Once in a while, a professional ballplayer comes along who loves the game so much he would play for nothing. Those fellows are rare these days. Most ballplayers now are businessmen more interested in how their investments are doing than what place their team is in or what their batting average happens to be. Some are more interested in their golf swing than their batting average. Steroids and other enhancers that some ballplayers use have made a mockery of the legendary records of Maris and Mantle. What was played in our front yard was far closer to Abner Doubleday's creation than what is performed in the big league ballparks today, and our games were more fun to watch.

Our version of baseball was simple on Enon Road in 1968. No one kept up with wins or losses, batting averages, errors, or any other vital statistic. Each day there were different teams, and unless the two oldest boys who were always captains were in a magnanimous mood, they would choose their teams. Every day the boys assembled around the bald spot that had been worn in the grass with the passing of summer. One boy would take a ball bat with the knob pointing to the sky and toss it straight up to the other captain, who would grab it with one hand. Quickly and with the experience of thousands of games, the boy who had thrown the bat would place his hand on the bat right above the other boy's hand. Then they would quickly move up the bat, hand over hand, until one boy had the knob covered with his hand. That meant he got the first choice, or he could defer and take the second and third choice, as fairness was a cardinal rule. Every boy wanted to win, but he wanted to win fairly with even teams. If all eight of the boys were there, David, the youngest, would usually bat for both teams, and one of the other boys would volunteer to pitch or play first base for both teams.

The unwritten rules stipulated that the team at bat had to provide the catcher. The catcher was expected to catch all pop ups and make any tags at the plate without showing favoritism towards his team, though all suspected that Little Dickie would cheat in his team's favor. He often missed pop ups that were easy, and that would always start a fight. The other fielders were usually a first/second baseman, a shortstop/third baseman, and one or two outfielders, depending if you needed to provide a pitcher or not. Sometimes only seven of the boys would show up to play. Little Dickie was often a "little sicky," as the boys would say, and would be confined inside the house with a sick stomach or a headache. One afternoon his brother Jimmy had reported that since Little Dickie had been complaining of a stomachache (likely brought on by eating a whole bag of old Easter candy he had found in the closet), Grandma had decreed that he must be constipated, and therefore, be in desperate need of an enema. That put Little Dickie on the disabled list all afternoon, but the next day he was back outside in the game. No one knew whether the enema had the desired effect, or if he had decided not to chance another one and came outside whether his stomach was hurting or not. Dickie had three hits that day. Some of the younger boys actually wondered if maybe they could somehow schedule one of the procedures. They had never had one and did not really know what it was all about. Of course no one ever discussed the details or what went on behind that closed door.

On this sweltering summer afternoon, the lords of baseball were gathered and were preparing to choose sides. The game the day before had ended in a vicious argument over whether Brad had tagged Jimmy out at second base or not. They almost came to blows and did come to some rather dramatic pushing. But at last Brad grabbed his ball—the only one we had—and went home mad. This was a new day, however, and all previous disagreements were forgotten. The game had to be played, and would be played, because word had gotten around that Jimmy had gotten a new baseball and glove from the Five and Dime in Ben Hill. He had oiled the glove down the night before, tied his baseball in it to shape it as his dad had shown him, and left it overnight. He was ready to try it out, but his older brother, Little Dickie, was jealous of Jimmy's new glove. Little Dickie commented that not even a new glove could help Jimmy's fielding, nor a new ball improve his hitting. Jimmy promptly banned Dickie from ever using his glove. That argument would only be solved by the high court of Mom and Dad later on that summer.

It was good that Jimmy had bought the new baseball because Brad had knocked the cover off of the old ball on a screaming line drive earlier that summer. The usual repair of an old baseball was to take Grandpa's black electrician's tape and tape all over it. It was just a ball of tightly wound string with black tape on it when we were finished, but it was a baseball. And if it got knocked into the bushes in foul territory, you hunted for it until you found it. The bats we used were badly worn and chipped, too, and taped on the handles with the same tape. We boys had all gone to an Atlanta Braves game the previous summer for "bat" night and had each received a bat. Now all that remained on the outside of each bat was part of the Louisville slugger name and the name of the Braves' star that had been on it. Little Dickie had a bat with Clete Boyer's name on it. Boyer was the Braves' third baseman and former New York Yankee legend. Near the end of his long, illustrious career, Boyer still had enough baseball in him to have boys like Little Dickie worship him and want a bat with the "Boyer" name on it. Boyer had hit 18 homeruns in 1967, with 120 hits and 58 RBI's, so Dickie revered the bat with the Boyer name. He almost worshipped it as if Clete himself had used it to hit a game winning homerun. It was no wonder that it was a month after he got it before he even used it in a game. Now, though, like the rest of our bats, it was worn, taped, dinged, and turning a darker shade of brown.

We soon had our teams chosen, this time with David, Uncle Gene's youngest, being allowed to bat for both teams. His outs would count. Earlier in the season when he did not hit very well, we did not count his outs. Now that he was hitting better, not only did his outs count, but we older boys no longer took his last swing. Most of us agreed that David was hitting better than Dickie, which Dickie, being older, vehemently denied. The two actually got into a shoving match one day when Dickie struck out for the third time that game. David, who had had two hits, one of which was a double, made the mistake of saying, "You swing like a girl." Those were fighting words, and Dickie tackled him on the spot. Had they been on different teams, it might have gotten out of hand. But as it was, we just gathered around and laughed until I finally drug David off Dickie's back.

There were no rules to choosing teams, though the oldest and best players were usually chosen first. Sometimes if one of the younger boys was hitting really well and able to catch fly balls, he might be chosen first. That day, though, the teams were basically divided equally between ages. David would bat for both teams.

"He swings both ways," Dickie called with a bawdy laugh. We all snickered, knowing that something of an adult nature had been said. But none, not even Dickie, knew what. David would bat first for each team, too. Dickie, being captain, had chosen first, so his team was in the field. My little brother, Andy, was on his team, as were Larry and Jimmy. On my team were cousins Brad and Stevie. Brad was a very young eleven but a hefty eleven. Some of us thought he might be the first to hit one over the road if he got his weight behind it. He did not run fast, so most of his doubles were only singles, and he had never hit an inside the park home run. He was just too slow. The kids all called him "Spanky" because of his size, and he hated the name. He wished we would call him "Hammer" or "Babe." But it stuck when Dickie called him Spanky, and for that, Brad hated Dickie deeply. Brad usually played first or pitcher, where he did not have to run much. He hated playing in the late afternoon, as sweat would pour off his body. But he played because he did love the game of baseball. He would go to bed every night, thinking of the great plays he had made or almost made, and he dreamed of being a slim, slick-fielding shortstop. He got up early every morning, ready for the day's game, wishing they could play under the lights in the cool of the evening. Even though Grandpa was an electrician, there were no thoughts by any of the parents of hanging lights in the front yard for us to play in the cooler evenings—at least not yet.

Our game uniforms were usually dirty t-shirts and blues jeans, which had been worn in every game that week. They were still unwashed and had dirty knees with holes in them from sliding into base at every opportunity. Only Little Dickie had ever worn short pants (which with his knobby knees he never should have done), and he seldom slid. One time in the excitement of the moment, trying to score a crucial run, he slid across home plate, which was nothing more than a flat rock on the hardened bald spot. He tore a ragged place from the skin on his knee. He was halfway to the house, limping and screaming, when he heard me yell, "Hey, Dickie, I bet Grandma gives enemas for busted knees, too." The shrill crying stopped immediately. He was soon back in the game, fighting back the tears with blood running down his leg. He turned in one of the gutsiest performances any of us had ever seen.

No one had cleats, and we had never even seen a pair up close. PF Flyers or Keds were the shoes of choice, or whichever ones that could "make you run faster and jump farther." Just to be different, Dickie wore his green tennis shoes that he had gotten at Paul Parrot's Shoes on the corner of Main Street in East Point. It was near Grandpa's electrical shop, called Fulton County Electric. The shoe store had a real live parrot in a cage in the front window. Though I never remember being in the store, I remember standing outside to look in at that parrot. We were not allowed, by a decree of motherhood, to play bare-footed, though our mothers had never been up to a game to see if their edict was being obeyed. The lack of stumped toes or cut feet must have been proof enough for them.

The game finally started with David swinging his Henry Aaron bat. Everyone on Dickie's team moved in close because David wouldn't hit it far. Little Dickie was pitching for his team because he hadn't hit anybody with a pitch in several games, and being the captain, it was always his choice. His brother, Jimmy, was playing first; my brother, Andy, played shortstop; and Larry, who was fast but whose fly ball catching ability was always suspect, was stationed in the outfield. Jimmy was the most athletic of the bunch and was sure to lead the summer front yard league in hitting by the next summer. He had natural abilities and was everything Brad wanted to be. But the great shame was that Jimmy, even as good as he was, did not love the game. Baseball was just something to do, so he did it. He did not live for the game like Brad. Brad lived for the game because it was the one time in the day when he could do something right—like get a hit with the bases loaded. It also got him away from his Dad, who often came home early in the afternoons.

Little Dickie was wearing long pants to give his knee a chance to heal, and he moved in close to pitch to little David. The object was not to strike David out, but to let him hit it where your team could get him out. Dickie's first pitch was a good one, and David smacked it hard in a long arc over second base, where his brother Larry was playing shallow. He easily made the catch. David hollered, "No fair. He's supposed to be playing in the outfield." But by the time he had hollered, Dickie had thrown the first pitch to Brad and the game moved on.

As Dickie wound up to throw the next pitch—always exaggerating his delivery to make sure everyone noticed his ability—Andy chattered out, "Hey, batter, batter, batter, swing." Those were the same words that are hollered wherever baseball is played, from front yard pick up games to every level of organized ball. No one knows who first uttered the now famous words, but they have been called so loud and so often that they are branded into the male psyche. They come out naturally even if the boys playing have never been to another ball game. Like the rule of the imaginary man, it is born into boys. It must be. I don't know, but I believe that anywhere boys gather to play baseball, in whatever country with whatever language, the call is the same.

As the pitch arrived at the plate, it was way outside. Brad stepped over to catch it and toss it back to the pitcher. The next pitch came in high and tight. Brad slapped a grounder to short, where Andy easily fielded and threw Brad out at first by two steps. Larry surprised everyone when Stevie hit a long shot over his head. Larry turned around and ran straight for the road, turning back around at the last instant for the ball to luckily fall into his outstretched glove. Dickie's team celebrated, not so much over the great catch, but over the three up and three down inning. It was an embarrassment to my team because seldom did a team not score at least one run in an inning (many times the final score would be 29–23 or 37–31). This time, however, Little Dickie was crowing about his pitching. "And I still didn't hit nobody" he said to anybody and everybody, but only nobody was listening.

Brad pitched for our team. I played shortstop, and Stevie was standing idly in the outfield. Dickie's team had to provide a first baseman since we were letting David bat for both teams. Again, since he was batting for both teams, David hit first, and again he swung at the first pitch, hitting it farther than he ever had before. It sailed into right field. Before Stevie could run it down and hurl it back screaming, "Foul ball," David had slid into third with a big, ear-to-ear grin. It was his first triple ever! Jimmy batted next but only managed a weak line drive to me at short. David, getting excited and forgetting he couldn't run on a line drive, ran for the plate despite the impassioned cries of his teammates. I ran over and tagged third for the double play before David could realize his mistake. "Rookie," we all thought. Andy hit next and grounded out to the pitcher, so we changed positions. We wondered what in the world was going on. After one inning the score was nothing to nothing, and already there had been a triple, a double play, and a great catch in the outfield

Little Dickie pitched to me next. I don't know what he was throwing or trying to throw, but the ball had movement on it that I had never seen before. I struck out. Dickie crowed, strutted around on the mound, and pumped his fist in the air. By the end of the inning, we still did not have a hit, and the score remained tied.

Dickie's team came to bat in the bottom of the inning. Before the dust settled, things were getting back to normal, as they had scored three runs. Dickie had gotten mad when thrown out at first and called me a "wuss," whatever that was. Stevie had a screaming fit when he dropped a fly ball, but after a hurried conference with him and a lot of cajoling, he stayed in the game and we played on. It was after our next at bat, when we again went three up and three down, that somebody realized that we did not have a hit. Dickie was throwing a "no-no," something never before done in front yard summer ball. It was something that was impossible to do; something Nolan Ryan couldn't do on his best day if pitching in our league. Yet Dickie was doing it. After four innings, with us hitless, it looked like Dickie was Cy Young, Tom Seaver, and Bob Gibson all rolled into the body of one knobby kneed Little Dickie Duncan—he of the torn knee and bright green tennis shoes. He pitched like a hall-of-famer inning after inning.

Inning after inning his team made heroic plays behind him; plays of legend; plays never before seen in that ball yard. Andy was playing like a man possessed. He not only caught all grounders, but several times dashed madly into short left field to catch fly balls before they dropped for hits. Jimmy dove at one grounder at first. While everyone held his breath to see if he could get up and get the runner, he rolled over and dove towards the bag, touching it just before David arrived. As we played, everyone knew this was the game we would remember forever. We all knew it was special; the game that we would talk about when we were old and gray and sitting around, reminiscing about the good old days.

The game hurried on. Brad settled down in his pitching, not allowing any more runs, as the lowest scoring game ever continued to develop. The harder we all tried to slug the ball, the more pop flies we hit. Both sides were trying mightily under the blazing sun to hit, to run, to score, or just reach base. Brad was pouring sweat and wiping constantly, but never complaining. Dickie pitched into the fifth and into the sixth and on into the seventh. No hits, no runs, no errors—a perfect game. By then, his strutting around on the mound had ceased. The sheer weight of what he was accomplishing was bearing down on him and beginning to take its toll. Dickie never responded well under stress. In that seventh inning, Brad came to bat with two outs. After two swinging strikes, Dickie laughed and yelled for all to hear, "Hey Spanky. Want me to pitch underhanded to you? You swing like your momma." A startled hush settled over the field as Brad glared out at Little Dickie.

Andy hurried to the mound from shortstop and reached down to pick up a handful of dirt. Looking up at Dickie, he said, "Dickie! Whatcha doin, man? Don't make him mad. He'll kill ya, if not during the game, then after it. Besides, he might quit and go home and the game would be over."

Dickie considered it for a moment. "I was just having some fun with him."

The game continued as Dickie once again went into his overly elaborate windup and hurled the ball towards home. With a grunt heard all over the field, Brad swung and missed. Strike three, out three. Seven no hit innings were in the books, if there had been books. By now, someone had run inside for a drink and spilled the word to Grandma about what was happening outside. Even though Grandma did not exactly understand it, she knew Dickie was doing something wonderful. Since those moments were rare, the phones rang. Soon, for the first time ever in Enon Road Front Yard Summer League play, parents wandered out to the shade trees near the field behind the first base line. Grandma brought out her folding chair. With her knitting, she sat down to watch the proceedings so she could give Grandpa a pitch-by-pitch account because he would certainly want to hear. By the time Dickie went out to pitch the eighth inning, an odd assortment of moms, aunts, an uncle or two, and assorted babies and toddlers were gathered in the shade. They did not know if they were allowed to cheer, or just what to do since they had never watched one of the games before. The mothers were all gratified to see no one was playing barefooted.

It was then that David, who had not had a hit since his triple, decided he had had enough. Not wanting the uncles, aunts, moms or Grandma to see him strikeout, he quit for the day, claiming he was too hot and about to pass out. Since David was only a minor player and did not play in the field, the game could go on without disruption. David's quitting dampened Dickie's spirit. David had been an easy out for him all day, and this meant one bigger boy to face more often. But Dickie, like all the greats down through the ages, rose to the occasion and was up to the task. When the eighth inning was done, the score was still 3–0, and Dickie's no hitter was still intact. History was being made with every pitch.

Dickie strutted to the mound, or the bald spot that we called the pitcher's mound, for the ninth inning. I stepped in against Dickie, determined to be the one who broke up the no hitter, but all I could do was hit a slow grounder to Dickie. He grabbed it and ran to first to beat me to the base, just to show off.

Brad was up next. He hit a hard grounder back at Little Dickie, who slapped it down, picked it up in a panic now, and threw wildly to first. "Safe," went the roar from the shade trees. Uncle Gene, Brad, Larry, and David's dad, with a beer in one hand, was quick to point out that though the perfect game was gone, it was still a no hitter because Dickie had made the error. Dickie had wanted the perfect game, but the no hitter was still shimmering out there just within his grasp, so he quickly agreed that he had made the error. There was no argument from us, and since a parent had violated the sacred rule of no parental involvement, we felt compelled to agree. Stevie was up next. He felt the pressure, but with a lot of encouragement, he stepped up to the plate and promptly swung at the first pitch. He, too, hit a groundball back to Dickie. Determined to atone for his error, Dickie made a great play on the ball, speared it, and turned to throw to second. Visions of a double play to end the game and still pitching to the minimum number of batters were upper most in his mind. Unfortunately, Andy was a step late getting to the bag—or stick as it really was—and in his haste, Dickie threw the ball too hard. It sailed into centerfield, where fortunately, Larry was alertly backing up the play. By the time the dust had settled though, runners were on second and third. All agreed it was another error by Dickie without any interference from the parental cheering section. So the no hitter was still in effect, but the shutout was definitely in danger, and it was my turn to hit.

Dickie had memories of the plastic bat and ball game earlier in the year where I had crushed one of his pitches into the night with a mighty blast that ultimately won the game. He wanted revenge. I wanted to continue my dominance over Dickie, which I had seen slipping that day. He had gotten me out all afternoon, several times on strikeouts.

Andy called time-out and trotted in from shortstop for another conference with Dickie. "Hey, Little Dick," he said as he got there. "What do you say to walking him to pitch to Brad next? That sets up a force at any base, and with Brad running, if we get another ground ball, we can end this thing with a double play."

Dickie was amazed. "But we have never walked anybody before."

Andy retorted, "Nobody's ever had a no-hitter in the ninth inning before, either."

"But how do we do it?" asked Dickie as he mulled it over. He was still thinking he could get me out for even more heroics. "We don't call balls and strikes. No umpire."

"Simple," responded Andy. "We just put him on. Intentional walk. We tell him we are walking him."

"Oh, really? Then you do it."

My younger brother looked over at me. He knew that if I had batted in that spot, that somehow, someway, I would have gotten on base. "OK," he said. "You can get Brad out, right?"

Dickie laughed. "Yeah. I've been getting lard butt out all day."

Andy looked hard at Dickie. "Dickie, you have been getting them all out all day long. Just don't let up now."

Andy called out to me as I stood at the plate, rubbing sand on the bat. "We're walking you. Take first."

Since this had never been done before, a five-minute argument ensued. Uncle Gene, now on his second beer, again interrupted and said that it was legal, as the intentional walk was a part of all organized ball. Much against my will, I walked slowly to first, still mad at Andy for what I knew was a brilliant strategic move. In the past, strategy had seldom been employed in our league. The bases were now loaded, with one out, and Brad was due up; a sweating, tired, mad, still seething Brad. The no hitter, the shutout, and the game were on the line.

Brad was the runner on third, so as the rules allowed, he called, "Imaginary man on third," and walked over to the old pine tree where our bats were laid out. He picked up Dickie's cherished Clete Boyer bat. Brad tapped it several times on the dirt to make sure it was sound. Then with vengeance pumping through his veins and registering on his face, he stood in against the man of the hour, Dickie Duncan. Dickie stared in at Brad, smiling evilly, and threw his best pitch of the day, which Brad swung at lamely and missed. Dickie hurled the next pitch, and Brad swung. He lined a foul ball that with one bounce landed in Grandma's lap, causing her to miss a stitch. Everyone wanted to laugh, but since it was Grandma, no one dared to until she laughed. Dickie and everyone else let out a gasp, just knowing the game would end right there. But everyone laughed when Grandma did—everyone, that is, except for Brad, who was staring madly at Dickie. Then, just before Dickie was to throw again, Brad stepped out of the batter's box and wiped his brow. He heard cries of, "Spanky, Spanky, don't you need a hanky," come from the field. Stepping back up to the plate, he swung the bat— once, twice—then settled in for the final pitch.

Little Dickie had Spanky right where he wanted him—two strikes. With a big crowd of parents looking on, the greatest feat ever in front yard baseball history was about to be accomplished. Dickie had visions of running and jumping into someone's arms in celebration. It would be great!

Brad looked over at his mom, and she blew him a kiss. He saw his dad standing there, raising his beer to him with a cheer. Facing Dickie, he nodded that he was ready. Dickie made his great big windup and fired the pitch. Every runner on every base started running as Brad swung from his heals; from his big butt; from every ounce of fat and muscle in him; from every bit of resentment against Dickie for calling him Spanky, and against his dad for all the beatings he had endured. Mostly he swung from his heart; a great heart that loved baseball; a heart that just loved playing the game; that loved being there in the moment; when one swing would make history, either way.

The bat crashed against the ball and shattered in Brad's hands. The ball flew out high and long, with Dickie watching in dumb amazement as it sailed over his head. Larry, in centerfield, turned and took off towards the road on a dead run, as mothers screamed, "Watch for cars!" Dashing up the incline and finally stopping at the edge of the road, he stared mutely as the ball sailed far and long over his head and smacked with a thud against the red clay of the far bank. There was total silence. Brad did not know what to do. He had stopped halfway to first base to watch the majestic homerun in amazement. The crowd was awed, wondering whether it was allowed to clap or not, or who should clap for whom, as each had at least one child on the field. The imaginary man on third saw the ball hit the far side of the road, and I think he screamed as he romped across home plate, his hand held high. Moments later, Stevie dashed in screaming to no one, jumping into the imaginary man's arms; a man who to him was as real as anyone in the assembled crowd. I then trotted across the plate, ignoring all the high fives as I turned to wait on Brad. He was circling the bases in a slow, professional homerun trot, finally realizing that he was the first and only one who had ever hit one over the road. He never remembered touching third base, and when he reached home, we all swarmed over him, shouting and screaming. Uncle Gene was there, pouring what was left of his beer all over Brad. He lifted him high in the air in a jubilant celebration that Dickie's mom found very distasteful. Brad's mom hurried over to kiss him, and Grandma was heard to say, "Wait until Grandpa hears about this." Wiping the beer out of his eyes, Brad looked out and saw with delight that Dickie was on his knees, utterly defeated once, for all, forever. There would be no more calls of "Spanky." Then Brad heard the sweetest words he had ever heard before. From way out at the road where Andy had gone to help find the ball came the cry, "Good hit, Bambino!"

Andy picked up the ball. Estimating the ball had flown about 250 feet, he threw it back in to no one in particular. Jimmy wandered over and picked it up, head bowed in disgust. He saw Dickie, still on his knees on the mound, holding part of his broken Boyer bat in his hands—the part that had flown out towards him when it splintered. Tears streamed down his face. Andy walked in from the outfield and looked down at Dickie.

"Well, there goes the no hitter and shutout," he said. "You ready for a relief pitcher?"

Dickie looked at him. "He broke my bat. He broke my Clete Boyer bat."

Andy dropped the ball at his feet, took the bat from him, and tossed it off the field. "Can't even tape that one back together. Just firewood now. The Bambino really did a number on it."

The rest of the game was a blur. Larry came in to pitch and got the final two outs. Brad went back to the mound in the bottom of the ninth and quickly got three outs without incident. The final score was 4–3. It would forever be remembered not that Little Dickie had almost pitched a no hitter, but that Brad, the Bambino, hit the first homerun over the road, and it was a grand slam to win a game!

Twenty-five years later at family reunions, the boys of Enon Road still talk about that moment in time. With almost a sense of reverence, they forever call Brad "Bambino."

CHAPTER TWELVE

⇒ *Moby Bass* ⇐

I went to bed that night dreaming about that wonderful, tremendous, exciting, best-ever baseball game. I woke with fishing on my mind, specifically, "The Fish," "The Grandpa," "Moby Bass," the fish of legend. Many fishermen claimed to have tangled with him over the years and lost. They bragged about it as if there were some distinct honor in belonging to the elite club of bass fishermen who had almost caught "The Grandpa," including Dale Wilson, my best friend's dad. Mr. Wilson supposedly hooked the giant bass one day while out in the middle of Grandpa's eight acre lake in the old aluminum boat that I still used. He battled it for two hours. Finally Mr. Wilson hollered that the fish had managed to tangle the line in some submerged tree limbs and there was nothing to do but to dive in after him. Dive in after him he did. I know, because I was on the shore and saw him do it. The bass may never have been on his hook; I am not sure. We boys really doubted that Mr. Wilson had hooked him because he was a man who was known to stretch the truth. We preferred to believe that he had been hung on that limb the whole time, but I did see him come up from the lake bottom with a hand full of seaweed and a mouth full of muddy water, shaking his head and sputtering, "I can't believe it! He got away. The biggest fish I have ever seen. What a monster."

So the legend of the monster bass in that lake grew in our minds; a bass that must shatter the world record; a bass that must clear twenty-five pounds if he cleared an ounce. I don't know how long bass live, but just the stories of this mystical fish had been going on for twenty years when I first took an interest in him. It was my ambition that year before I reached the seventh grade to catch that mystical fish and prove my manhood. I continued walking down to the lake every chance I got. I carried my faithful Zebco 33 attached to the rod that had been dubbed "The Lunker Stick," and my trusty .22 rifle or shotgun in one hand. My other hand held Grandpa's old, worn-out but huge tackle box and the boat paddle.

It had been a hot summer since school was out. It was one of the ones in the South when the temperature is already 80 degrees when the sun comes up. The humidity is so thick, the air hangs there, and you almost have to grab it and stuff it into your mouth just to inhale. On many afternoons you could count on a thunderstorm around 3:00, the time of day when the atmosphere gets so hot that it simply can not stand it any longer and explodes at some upper stratospheric level. The result is a "gully washer," or the more ominous "frog strangler." I had seen plenty of gully washers in my time, and I have seen washed out ruts on the road to the lake that proved many of these downpours over the years, but I still haven't seen a frog strangled by the rain. We struggled to get our afternoon ballgames in some days, and many times my fishing excursions were cut short or rained out altogether. It was the rule, for obvious reasons, that no one could be out on that lake in the aluminum boat during a storm. I did get caught out a time or two. A storm would rumble in faster than I had realized, with lightning popping all around. I expected to be struck dead or blinded at any moment as I paddled against that fierce wind. Trying to juggle my summer schedule was difficult with the bike riding, fishing, baseball, and nighttime plastic bat and ball games coming so close together. I usually was able to get down to the lake to fish for "Moby Bass" sometime during the week, often after supper depending on which night Little Dickie's favorite television shows came on. We never played ball during his programs. On the nights when I did get to the lake after supper, the rule was "be home before dark". I did not really want to get caught out after dark, anyway. That meant having to walk home through the pasture and the pine thickets by myself. That was frightening, especially after my Papa had told me stories of his childhood when his mom warned him to get home before dark or "Old Raw Head and Bloody Bones" might get him. I sure didn't want to meet some raw headed, bloody boned fellow at night by myself.

After breakfast on this hot and dense day, I told Mom I was going fishing. With her usual "be careful," followed closely by "don't slam the door" as it banged with a vengeance behind me, I was soon walking with my equipment through the tan colored sage brush waving in the pasture. Then I hurried along the cow trail where it finally hit the main road that ran down from Grandpa's house. Reaching the lake, I soon had the boat turned over once again. With my shirt off, I paddled to the shallow end of the lake. I expected the bass to be in the shallow water in the cool of the morning, though the sun was now shining and heating up the water rapidly. This end of the lake—the end away from the dam—was full of submerged stumps that usually made their appearance during droughts as the lake level dropped. Knowing from long experience where each and every stump and underwater log or limb was, I expertly tossed the plastic worm towards the "cover" again and again, with no strikes, no bumps, nothing. I paddled from shore to shore, casting and paddling, reeling and casting, and reeling and paddling some more, but the fish were not biting. After an hour or so, I let the boat drift down to the deeper end where the dam and the cattails were, just to make my obligatory cast into the lair of the "Monster." Still nothing. Sighing deeply, I began paddling towards shore and soon was hiking back home. Minutes after I had turned the boat over and left the bank of the lake, the cattails parted as a monster began his morning forage for breakfast in deep water.

CHAPTER THIRTEEN

⇒ *The New Ball Field* ⇐

I t was not very long after that magnificent baseball game that the adults decided we needed a real ball field; some place that had an actual infield, bases and a real back stop. I think the mothers were motivated by their desire to get us away from playing near the road. That had always made them nervous. The fathers were motivated by the dreams of their sons becoming major league stars. After that game, they began to believe that for some of us, it just might be possible.

The question uppermost in their minds, however, was where could they put a new ball field? It had to be near enough to the houses for us to hear our moms call us home, and it needed to be someplace flat with plenty of room for a homerun. We boys had no clue what was in their minds until Dad, Uncle Richard, and Uncle Gene took us for a walk late one evening. They gathered us up, and we followed behind them through the gate and down the pasture road towards the barn. We reached the giant mulberry tree on the left and the barn up on the hill to the right, chattering lots of questions as to what this excursion was about. The dads turned left across the pasture and walked past old piles of cow manure until they reached a pine thicket. Turning us around to look back towards the barn and mulberry tree, my dad said, "Well, boys, what do you think?"

"About what?" Little Dickie asked the question we were all wondering.

"Your new ball field," Uncle Richard responded proudly.

We all began to talk at once and were whooping and hollering until they finally settled us down. "We have talked to Grandpa," my dad began, "and we think this would be a great place to put a ball field for you boys. Home plate would be back here. We would cut out those little trees and put in a backstop. We are talking about even putting a fence up in the outfield and," Dad paused for dramatic effect, "Grandpa even said he thought we could put in some lights!"

We all stood mesmerized. Our minds flew to the moment when we would play under the lights—all night long if we wanted—hitting homeruns over the fence and one day past the mulberry tree. It would be great! What a dream. We rushed our dads as one mob and swarmed them to the ground in jubiliation, as if we had just won the World Series. We celebrated for a long time, rolling in the grass on our dads, wrestling them and then each other. Finally jumping up, we ran imaginary bases and slammed imaginary homeruns until the dark began to descend. We couldn't believe it. We were going to have a ball field. The boys of Enon Road were going to have a ball field. We all went to bed that night with visions of our ball field—more grand than our dads had in mind, I am sure. But whatever the result, we knew it would exceed whatever we could dream. It would be better than playing in the front yard with the pecan trees in the way.

The next Saturday, we boys met down at the mulberry tree and mulled around in the wet grass for a while, waiting on our dads to show up. It was as if we thought that by lunch time the field would be complete, and by early noon we could be playing ball. We had no conception of time. Time to us was like it is to God, who sees a day as a thousand years and a thousand years as a day. We didn't measure time in minutes or seconds. None of us usually wore a watch, but as we waited patiently there by the tree, we began to understand eternity. Finally, after two eternities had passed, Dickie had to go to the bathroom and ran off towards the house, bare legs shinning in the morning sun.

Brad laughed when Dickie was out of earshot. "He's got the bladder of a girl," he suggested, and we all laughed. I pulled a blade of sagebrush, stripped it down, and stuck it between my teeth. Walking toward where home plate would be, I began marking off lengths to bases and trying to figure just how the field would be aligned.

Before long, Dickie reappeared looking dejected. "There ain't going to be no ball field built today," he said. Stevie, who had been hanging out with us and doing really well, had a look of disbelief on his face. Dickie continued, "Dad said they have to get somebody over here to bush hog it first. If they can get that done this week, then maybe next Saturday we can work on it." Stevie cried out in frustration and began stalking to the house with his head hung down.

We were disappointed, but we sat down in the wet grass and talked at great lengths about the infield. One of us even suggested we could have real bases if Grandma would take some old material and make them for us. We wondered, too, if we would have dugouts. We all agreed that might be asking too much. Finally we wandered off back towards our homes to watch what was left of Saturday morning cartoons—all except Dickie, that is. Just before going through the gate, I looked back to the field. Where the pitcher's mound would be, I saw Dickie going into a full windup and hurling an imaginary baseball to his imaginary catcher. I watched for some minutes, mesmerized by Dickie's windup, delivery, and pitching. He must have been having a great game from the way he was gesticulating in victory, often pumping his hands high. Maybe he was reliving "The Game" but with a different outcome this time; an outcome where he struck out the side to save his no hitter. It was just like Dickie. We didn't have the field built yet and he already had a ballgame going. I was jealous that I hadn't thought of it first.

The man with the bush hog did not come that week, nor the next. We realized that summer was quickly passing away. If we didn't care about time in minutes or days, we did care a lot about it in terms of seasons. Summer, which was our favorite because school was out, would soon be gone. We didn't play as much front yard ball now because the promise of the new field made our front yard ball yard seem so inconvenient with the trees in the way and the sticks for bases. Many afternoons found us wandering aimlessly down at the mulberry tree, wondering if we could somehow cut the grass, but it was just too high. Not able to wait, we did hit some fly balls to check on the right distance for the fence. We were pleased that a slight rise that rimmed the outfield would be just perfect for the outfield fence.

We questioned our dads, and they said to be patient.

We mentioned it to Grandpa and took him down to look it over. The excitement came back until Grandpa said that it would take a lot of work and maybe a little more money than we thought. It was doable, he said, especially since he had gotten rid of his last cows, so he would talk it over with our dads. When that did not speed things up, we attacked our moms and tried to get them to get our dads to work on the project, but that did not help, either.

In the end, nothing was ever said that it wouldn't be built, but it just never got built. The man with the bush hog never came, and our dads never did anything more than just talk about it. I know they meant well and had a dream of a ball field there for their boys. As I have learned since, sometimes the realities of life interfere with our dreams. The best laid plans and ideas sometimes are pushed aside and forgotten in the every day humdrum business of life. Uncle Gene was still recuperating from his surgery and was on half days at work. He came home too exhausted to even think about working on some ball field. Uncle Richard often worked late and when he did get home, he scurried out to his shop immediately after supper to tinker on some engine. Daddy worked the nightshift, so he was leaving home in the late afternoon. He often worked Saturdays, too. When he was off, he spent his time cutting his own yard or doing odd jobs for Mom. So it was just never done, as good an idea as it was.

Late one evening I came walking back up from the lake, disappointed from my latest failure to catch "The Grandpa." I saw Dickie, once again on the mound. He was firing imaginary fastballs to an imaginary hitter, hearing the roars of an imaginary crowd. I laid my fishing gear down and walked through the ankle high grass into what would have been center field. "Hey, Little Dick," I hollered, pounding an imaginary glove. "Let him hit. He can't get it past me." Dickie looked back at me, surprised at first, but then he nodded.

"Get ready," he answered. "The bases are loaded. Hank Aaron is up with two outs in the ninth, and I haven't gotten him out yet today. We only got a two run lead."

With that he turned and looked into his catcher as 35,000 people stood and roared in anticipation of this match up. This game would be talked about forever, no matter how it turned out. This was one of legend; one for history; one for the books; one for young boys to tell their grandsons one day. Shaking off one sign, Dickie finally got the one he wanted, whirled, and fired.

"Strike one," the umpire shouted, and the crowd roared in approval. Dickie got the next sign, rocked, and fired. Hammerin Hank swung, but the ball was past him. The crowd was wild and the noise deafening. Dickie walked off the back of the mound. He was playing the moment for all it was worth and enjoying every second. Finally, walking slowly back up the hill, he leaned over for the sign. An evil snarl of hatred curled his upper lip. He wound up and hurled his fastest pitch yet.

I heard the crack of the bat and instinctively ran to where I knew the ball would have to be. Dickie whipped around as it soared by him. It gained altitude and headed for the gap. Within two steps I was in a full gallop, speeding towards the deepest part of the ballpark. I heard nothing. I saw nothing but a white sphere as it tried to sail by me. I felt nothing. I could not feel my feet touching the earth, and indeed I felt like I was flying. Reaching up with my glove and diving with body fully extended,

I heard the baseball hit leather at almost the same time I hit the ground with a thud. I skidded through the wet grass, turning on to my right shoulder to break the skid. There was total silence as I lay there. Every person in the crowd held their breath, waiting on the umpires call. Dickie was peering through the gathering gloom. Reaching into the glove, I felt the sweetest piece of cowhide I had ever touched. Pulling the ball out, I held it aloft, and the umpire signaled, "Out!"

Dickie jumped for joy and raced for me. The crowd released its breath, sucked in deep, and let out a roar that cracked windows in homes three miles away. Within seconds Dickie was jumping into my arms like it was the last game of the World Series—and who knows, but it might have been. Hank shook his head and melted into the shadows. "Great catch," Dickie laughed. "I've never seen one like it. You saved the day."

I finally stood up and brushed myself off. "No, Dick," I said. "It was your game. You kept him in the ballpark. All I had to do was catch it. Great game, man." With that, I turned to pick up my fishing equipment, and Dickie went skipping up the road towards home. I stood in wonder at what had just happened. The field was darkened now, but somehow I felt that I had caught that ball. Reaching down to pick up my fishing rod, I was stunned when I found a baseball still in my hand. Now how had that gotten there?

The field may never have been built, but we had our greatest games ever there. Hank Aaron came to play, as did Eddie Matthews, Rico Carty, Felipe Alou, and many others of our favorite Braves. Ernie Banks of the Cubs played there, and Bob Gibson pitched there, as did Denny

McClain and Don Drysdale. Maury Wills stole seven bases in one game, and Boog Powell hits five homeruns in another. Al Kaline made catch after catch (but none as good as mine). All-Star games and World Series were held there weekly. Dickie and Baltimore Oriole Manager Earl Weaver had some famous arguments. Once even Stevie got involved, but Earl did not stand a chance against Stevie. When Earl tried to kick dirt on Stevie's feet, Stevie kicked old cow manure back.

We eventually went back to playing ball in the front yard. The field by the mulberry tree continued to grow so that it was soon overgrown with briars and we could no longer go there. Years later, Little Dickie was still talking about my catch. I still wonder.

CHAPTER FOURTEEN

⋙ *The Legacy* ⋘

One evening after supper, before I could dash out to our nightly plastic bat and ball game (which sometimes was broken up when we took a notion to catch lightning bugs instead), Mom called us all into the living room with some exciting news. Grandma and Grandpa McKenzie, Mom's grandparents and my ancient great-grandparents, were making the trip up from Tampa to visit with Grandma and Grandpa for a week. They wanted especially to spend some time with us. It was to be, Mom said in hushed, awed tones, their last trip because they were both in their later eighties and beginning to have some health problems. Long car rides were getting to be too much for them.

We had visited Grandma McKenzie the previous summer on our vacation. I remembered her for her shock of white hair, and especially for her eyes that seemed to dance and sparkle when she spoke. Devoutly religious, she had mothered six children—five that were still living—including my grandma and her brother Frankie. Frankie drove his parents to Atlanta and would be driving them back to Tampa. This was a cause for some concern amongst the adults because he was known to "love the bottle overly much," as Grandma had put it once. He had never been the best of drivers.

Grandpa "Robert" McKenzie was a native Scotsman. He had emigrated from Edinburgh as a young man when he grew tired of working in a morgue amongst the dead. (One of the stories he told us was of dead people moaning and actually sitting up while he worked there.) He traveled across America to South Dakota, where he got a job on a farm working with steam-powered tractors. While standing in a neighbor's yard one afternoon, he heard a giggle come from above him. He looked up to the roof of the farm house and saw two beautiful legs dangling over the side. A female face with long, wavy hair and blue eyes soon appeared, and Grandpa McKenzie knew he was looking at his future wife. Sarah Elder was introduced by her father. It wasn't long before Robert McKenzie soon appeared back at that farm to ask her father's permission to court the lovely daughter.

They married in the spring and then spent many years traveling the northern United States and Canada as they worked from farm to farm repairing farm equipment. Their daughter Ruby, who would be my grandma, was born in a tent outside of Alberta, Canada, near an Indian reservation. Robert had ridden a horse over to the reservation to get a woman to come and help deliver the baby.

With the children beginning to grow, they migrated south, finally settling in Tampa where Robert got a job with the railroad. Now retired, he loved nothing better than to sit on the porch in the evenings and play "Aggravation," a board game with marbles and dice. They had their own homemade board made of plywood. It was complete with holes scooped out to hold the marbles as they were moved around the board, and edges on the board to keep the dice from rolling off. It had to be one of the original "Aggrava-tion" boards that is now sold in stores. Near the end of his long and happy life, the tall and still muscular Grandpa McKenzie would gather us boys around him and regale us with tales from his early years in Scotland. He went into great detail as if he were passing on a legacy, the passing of which we soon realized was one of his main reasons for coming to Georgia. He came to visit his daughter and grandchildren, but he was more interested in us boys and spent a lot of time around us. I never understood it, but he even made us learn what he called the "Scottish" alpha-bet, which went something like this: "ABC DEBED LM NOD Q TO FY W XY ZOD." He would repeat that, and he would laugh as we tried to rehearse and remember it. Surprisingly, it was Stevie who picked up on it the quick-est. Soon he was boring everyone to tears by quoting it at least 100 times a day, time after time after time.

Uncle Frankie, Grandma's baby brother and only son of Sarah and Robert McKenzie, had driven his parents to Atlanta. He was another figure that we boys loved to be around. He still lived with his parents, had never married, and had never really held down a job. We never saw him without a bottle of Pabst Blue Ribbon beer in his hand. My mom worried about his bad influence, but other than his drinking, he was a kindly gentleman. He had enough of his dad in him that he loved nothing better than to sit around and tell us boys stories of days long past and adventures he had. When we related them to Mom, she snorted and said the only adventure Uncle Frankie ever had was running out of beer and having to hurry down to the beer joint to get some more. Uncle Frankie sat on the porch in the evenings and cheered us on as we played plastic bat and ball. Once he even came out to take a couple of swings himself. I was the honored one who got to pitch to him. It was my job not to strike him out but to let him hit it, which he did. After he hit one so hard that it busted both the bat and the ball, Grandma McKenzie would not allow him to play with us anymore.

I don't know how the Duncans managed that week. With their family and Grandma and Grandpa already living in the house, they then had to find beds and bedrooms for their guests. I did notice that Uncle Richard worked later most evenings that week. 1968 was still a time when relatives went out of their way to house other relatives. They did not think it inconvenient to care for them; nor did the visiting relatives think it inconvenient to visit for a week or longer.

In my earlier years before the Duncans moved in with Grandma and Grandpa, Grandpa's mother, whom everyone called "Granny," often stayed with Grandma and Grandpa. She was a short, roly-poly-looking woman with the gray hair that we boys noticed on most old people. If you had gray hair, we thought you were old. When someone turned 50, we thought the person was over the hill. When someone reached 60 we thought the person was ancient. So to be around "living fossils," as Dickie said one day of the great-grandparents McKenzie, was exciting. Granny lived with her children on a three month rotating basis. Thoughts of putting her in a nursing home were never considered. It was her children's responsibility to provide for her needs until death, and they did just that. Grandpa especially made sure that she had everything she needed or wanted, even bringing her to his house after she had fallen and broken her hip. Grandma did not work outside the home, so she provided the care that was needed. One tragic thing that America lost in the last century was the stay at home mother. When moms were forced into the work place to provide for their families, childcare was often provided by friends, strangers, or daycare nurseries. The loss of mom at home also meant there was no one there to care for the aging parents, so more nursing homes sprang up, and more people who hated the thought were placed in them out of need. The greatest thing a senior can hope for is to live well and then to die before being committed to one of those dreaded facilities.

All too soon the week was over, and Grandma and Grandpa McKenzie and Uncle Frankie were set to leave. With kisses and waves all around, they loaded into their car, and we watched as they drove away. To me it was like history passing away before my eyes; like an important part of me had just left with them. What I realize now is that rather than part of me leaving, an important part of them had been left behind in us, a part that we can still remember, laugh about, and talk about today. Some day I hope to visit my great-grand kids and leave my legacy in their hearts. When I do, I will tell them about the McKenzies. I will tell them how they met in the wheat fields of South Dakota and how they were part of what made America strong. What was passed to me, I must pass on so that their legacy will live in yet another generation.

Just after Christmas, we got the sad news that Grandpa McKenzie had died of a sudden heart attack after a rousing game of "Aggravation." Grandma McKenzie lived for many more years, until she was 98. She was always able to live with one of her daughters in the Tampa area. She was in church every Sunday up until the day she died.

CHAPTER FIFTEEN

⤜ *VBS* ⤚

V acation Bible School was one of the most exciting adventures for us in any summer. It came late in June at the little country church where we all attended. We loved to go to it for the running and ripping with the other kids, the games we would play, the great crafts we would make—like shoe shine kits that we actually got to nail together and then paint—and especially for the refreshments of grape Kool-aid and cookies. I can still taste the grape drink and wonder that my upper lip is not stained permanently purple from the gallons of the stuff that I drank. Bible lessons came in there somewhere, but those were just tolerated so we could do the other stuff. We started every morning at 9:00 am sharp, not at 8:57 or 9:02, but at 9:00. We lined up in front of the church, ready to march in to the sound of the old, clangy piano playing the theme song. (I am not sure if it was the piano or the piano player that was so off key.) Two of the older kids in the senior high class got to hold the flags at the head of the two columns—the Christian flag on one side and the American flag on the other. One of the little kids carried the big, old church Bible that some saint in history unre-membered donated to the church for the perpetual mem-ory of some now long forgotten loved one. Us middle aged kids didn't get to do anything special but march in, but that was neat enough to get us excited, anyway. As usual,

Little Dickie was beside me. His hair was slicked down, knobby knees showing bravely just above the white socks that were pulled way up on his calf; his feet stuck down into his shining Sunday shoes. He stayed as far away from Brad as possible, because Brad was making sure everyone had heard the story of his great homerun blast over the road off of Dickie. The piano clanged out, and we felt the line of kids surge ahead, up the cement steps and into the redbrick church building. We sang "Walking with Jesus," the chorus that was our VBS theme year after year. The VBS director had tried to use a publishing company VBS song one year just to be different, but the kids would not move until the pianist finally started playing "Walking with Jesus." Then we all began marching in.

With the theme song completed, we remained standing for the pledge to the American flag, the pledge to the Christian flag (which we didn't know so well), and then finally the pledge to the Bible, which none of us could remember except for the light unto our feet—or was it lamp? After that, the preacher, dressed in short sleeved white shirt and tie but without his Sunday coat so he would look less formal, led us in singing some old time camp type choruses without the piano, which we all sang loudly. We even made the hand motions to "Rolled Away, Rolled Away, Rolled Away." After we got settled down from the singing, the preacher started talking about our missionaries. He told us how we needed to raise $20 for them so they could buy a goat for the African village they were in. That one goat would give the whole village milk every day. All us Enon Road cousins and brothers had shiny quarters in our pockets that Grandma had given us just for this occasion. As the collection plate was passed, we all looked hard at each other to make sure everyone was giving his quarter. We especially watched Dickie, who had been known to keep his Sunday school offering from time to time. He would stash it in a secret place at home, which may account for his coming up with the money to buy that dirty magazine.

Bible classes with some of the mothers were next. I was always glad when I knew my mom would be teaching me because she could really keep you interested in the lesson. She had a way of presenting it so that when you left, you wanted to come back for more. Unfortunately, that year we were juniors, and juniors got Old Mrs. Sinclair, a dear lady. She had been teaching Sunday school and VBS for over 40 years. She still taught like she did 40 years earlier. Her teaching was so boring that she almost put us to sleep, even when talking about fun subjects such as Gideon and his gang of 300. She did get our attention teaching about Samson killing all those guys with a donkey jawbone, except she said it was the jawbone of an ass. When she said that, all the little girls gasped, and we boys busted out laughing because you just didn't say "ass" in mixed company. Mrs. Sinclair had a big mole on the side of her chin that had a long, black hair growing out of it. When she talked, the mole jiggled up and down, which helped keep our attention.

With our class finished, we charged outside to run and rip in the graveled parking lot in the shade of the giant oak trees. We played chase or freeze tag, even letting the bolder girls play from time to time. Every time we played, though, you could count on Dickie pulling a muscle, skinning a knee, bruising his shin, or doing something to get attention. Red Rover was the game of choice one day. We did not let Dickie play because his arms were so thin that he would break a bone when we chanted to send someone "right over." The person would always run right at Dickie and break the line. After recess, we all gathered in the shade of one of the oak trees by the old well where two tables were set up and loaded with Kool-aid and cookies. The preacher always managed to show up right on time. He would say a loud, long prayer, blessing every child by name and every cookie we were anxious to consume. I opened my eyes to see what the other kids were doing during this sermon-length prayer. I was astonished to catch Dickie with his hand on the table and a cookie already in his mouth. He had his eyes closed, so it was fair and really a brilliant ploy, though I never admitted it to him. After the preacher finally said "Amen," we surged towards the table but were further hindered by the preacher, who bellowed, "Back up, boys. Where's your manners? Ladies first. Come on, ladies. Refreshment time." We couldn't believe it, as some of the girls were as big as we were, wore jeans like we did, and were meaner than most of us. We shouldn't have been polite to them because they would beat us up if they caught us being polite to them at any other time.

When all the cookies were eaten and the grape drink was still showing on our upper lips, we hurried towards the basement where the crafts were set up with Mr. George Scarborough. He was a big, tall carpenter who walked with a limp that he earned from a jeep wreck in the war. He was a deacon in the church, and one day he admitted that he got the injured leg because he wrecked while driving drunk. We all gasped, but there it was. He proclaimed the evil of the bottle and encouraged us never to drink. That year we came in expecting and hoping to do something wonderful like the shoe shine kits of the year before. But we were truly amazed when we walked into the small, dark, damp basement, because Mr. Scarborough had bird houses for us to build. He had spent the whole past year collecting the lumber, cutting it into the proper pieces, and putting together just the right number of nails. Monday was the best day because we got to use sand paper and spent the whole 45 minutes sanding the edges and the ends. When we left, we couldn't wait to get back the next morning and nail the pieces together.

Leaving the basement, we dashed back around front for the closing exercise to find moms already beginning to park along the side of the road to pick up their children. Back inside the sanctuary, the preacher gave us the totals for the day, announcing the offering total of $7.65. The boys had outnumbered the girls by only two. Hearing that, the girls were determined to bring all their friends to outnumber the boys the next day. It did not make any difference to us Enon Road boys because we were the only boys we knew, other than our friends at church who were already there, anyway. After another long prayer, the preacher dismissed us, and we hurried outside to climb inside Grandma's old Plymouth with the fins on the back. She took us home because Mom stayed behind to clean up and get ready for the next day.

CHAPTER SIXTEEN

➤ Hill No. 121 ⇐

"**I**ncoming!" Andy screamed, but it was too late. The mortar shell exploded twenty yards away to my right. It sent shrapnel in all directions and caused the whole platoon to dive for cover in the trees and bushes at the foot of the hill. We had been ambushed in our attempt to retake Hill No. 121, which Charlie Company had lost the day before in a vicious late-morning firefight. I heard moaning from the edge of the trees. I looked over and saw Dickie lying there, writhing in pain with what looked like his leg half blown off. If anybody was going to get it, I knew it would be him. It was always him.

He wasn't the first Vietnam casualty, and he wouldn't be the last in what was fast becoming a hopeless war, a no-win situation; a war being fought on the streets of the United States capital as well as in the hills and jungles of Vietnam. It was a war with young boys dying horribly, but dying bravely. Many died because their government had sent them and they had no other choice but to be men, to be Americans, and to be obedient. It was a war that would eventually end with over 55,000 dead, and many times that in broken hearts, dreams, and shattered lives. It would end with moms and dads forever changed by the loss of that beloved son who would never come home again. For many, there would never, ever be closure. They, too, would become casualties of the war, but nameless and forgotten ones. It was a war that had started with lofty ideals of crushing communism in what was called a free South Vietnam, but in what was really a feudal kingdom with wicked landlords. Thousands protested all over America, fighting police and the National Guard. Some were even gunned down on college campuses, where much of the rebellion to the war was centered.

The boys of Enon Road were oblivious to all of this civil unrest. All we knew was that our fellow Americans were being killed in combat, and that was where we belonged. This mission of retaking Hill No. 121 had been in the planning stages all morning. We had discussed the best options for attack and pored over the maps that we had drawn up the night before. The lush green foliage closed around us as we snuck up the trail, trying to remain hidden as we approached our objective. Andy and Brad were out front on recon, and the rest of the platoon had fanned out along the brush line. We started up the incline, hugging the ground, and flitting from tree to tree and bush to bush. I took out my binoculars and scanned the area, but I could see nothing for the dense forest. Hearing a whistle from up ahead, we dropped to the ground onto our bellies, hardly daring to look up. We held our collective breaths as an enemy patrol passed just below us. The stinking, hated Viet Cong finally walked out of sight. Andy and Brad came crawling hurriedly back towards us with looks of disgust and fear on their faces. It was then that the mortar blast came in.

Hearing his screams, I snaked it over to Dickie through the terror and mayhem of the incoming shells. Grenades fell around us. Small arms fire peppered the trees as the VC patrol located us and tried to charge our position. A machine gun up on the hill began spitting out destruction all around us, keeping us pinned down. "Cover me," I hollered to Andy. He rolled over and opened up with his BAR, momentarily silencing the machine gun above us and sending the charging VC scurrying for protection. Managing to get to Dickie, I grabbed him and drug him down a gully and behind a tree, out of the line of fire. The rest of the guys in the platoon swung into action as they ripped the hill in front of them with grenades and rifle fire, shooting anything that moved.

Looking down at the moaning Dickie, I saw his ashen face and quivering, pale lips and knew he was in trouble as he mumbled over and over, "Momma, Momma." He was losing blood—lots of it—and there was no medic to help. There was little I could do but watch him die right there before my eyes. Despite everything, despite the great training we had endured, the great planning we had gone through and despite the fact that we had the power of the greatest nation ever on the face of the earth behind us, there was nothing that I could do to help but be there with him.

"Hang on, Dick," I said frantically as the roar of war continued around us. "Help is coming, man." Seeing Jimmy just up the hill to my right, I screamed for him to radio for a medivac helicopter. Jimmy was on his knees, where he had been fighting his own personal war. Gooks were stacked up around him like cordwood. I saw a bloody knife in his hand, a horrible gash across his forehead. The VC had tried to overrun his position, so he had been fighting hand to hand, using knife, bayonet, hands, and anything he could grasp and swing like a club. We had come a long way from front yard baseball when hitting baseballs was our only challenge.

"Radio's dead!" he screamed over the roar. "We can't stay here, Captain. We've got to get back to our LZ." He looked at me, waiting on me to give the word to fall back. But I wasn't moving—not yet. We still had a hill to take, and we weren't leaving until we had.

Those were my orders, and we were going to obey them or die trying.

Dickie moaned again. Time was indeed running out. Larry lay wounded near Jimmy, where he had tried to get to Jimmy to help him. Brad had been hit and lay behind a tree, out of action. David was crawling to get to Larry, and I saw him suddenly go still. Andy was still firing away, but had been hit several times. We were being decimated and had no way to call for reinforcements.

"Give me my weapon," Dickie grimaced. "I ain't dying. Not here. Not today. Not on this stinkin' hill."

I pushed his M16 onto his chest where he grabbed it and held tight.

It was in that moment that I heard his mom calling. "Dickie! Jimmy! Lunchtime." I saw the look that came into Dickie's eyes, and I knew immediately what would happen next. With a rebel yell on his lips, Dickie staggered up. Ignoring his pain, he charged straight up the hill into the face of death, hell and the grave, right into the face of the withering fire, shooting and throwing grenades as he ran. It was the gutsiest, craziest, wildest charge I had ever seen, and it was glorious! Seeing this extraordinary courage, I jumped to my feet and stormed right up the hill after Dickie. I waved for the platoon to follow, screaming encouragement as I went. Somehow, they all managed to get to their feet, find weapons, and charge after us, adrenalin rushing through one and all. Andy lumbered along with his big weapon, blood gushing for half a dozen wounds. He fired from his hip as he ran. Brad pulled himself up, and with a look of utter fearlessness, joined the charge up worthless Hill No. 121. Jimmy grabbed a gook weapon, pulled Larry and David to their feet, and they all followed Dickie's mad dash, one and all defying death and daring the enemy to stop us. In a wild, mad attack, we charged up and over the enemy position, wiping out the Viet Cong garrison and retaking Hill No. 121, just in the nick of time. Looking around and back down the hill and realizing what we had just accomplished, we collapsed on the ground in amazement at Dickie's guts. We all agreed it was the most heroic piece of work that we had ever seen and voted unanimously to meet back on top of the hill right after lunch to award Dickie the "Silver Cross" with a "V" for valor. We marched off that hill in single file. Dickie was still limping but insisted that he come off that hill without help. We marched out of those woods with our heads held high. We were deliriously happy; proud to be Americans, proud to have fought with Dickie, and proud to have taken our objective, Hill No. 121. Unfortunately, Mom had other plans for me, and I missed the awards ceremony. I understand that it was a beauty, complete with the national anthem and medals for all. I spent the rest of the afternoon cutting the front yard.

That night just after supper, as I passed by the television in the living room, I heard Walter Cronkite, the newsman, reporting from Vietnam. "The Viet Cong retook Hill No. 121 late this afternoon, taking heavy casualties with 42 killed, but killing 19 Americans and wounding 36 others in the fierce battle for this critical piece of bloody ground ... ... however, reports from command headquarters are that a counterattack to retake the hill will come soon."

CHAPTER SEVENTEEN

➣ *Down Strawberry Mountain* ➢

The Christmas of 1967 had been a spectacular one for the boys of Enon Road. It was the Christmas of the mini-bike, small motorcycles that were just the right size to zip around the yard or ride down to the lake. Dickie and his brother Jimmy each got one, and my brother Andy got one. It was an orange one that would almost climb a tree, or so we had been told. Christmas Day was an exciting time for the boys. As soon as the sun came up, the machines were cranked, and the family gathered in the front yard to watch the boys of Enon Road come of age on their motorized bikes. When I heard that Dickie had gotten the biggest one—a bright blue one—I knew he was no longer Little Dickie, but Dangerous Dickie or Deadly Dickie, even. I knew that my days of group leadership were definitely about over, as I would never be able to keep up with the boys as they zoomed around the woods on these things. Standing in the yard in what was right field in summer and the end zone for football in the winter, we watched as Dickie, Jimmy and Andy raced around. With their helmets on, they carefully tested the bikes at first, then opened them up to see how fast they would go. It wasn't until Dickie hit the curve where we were standing at full speed that we realized what a foolish thing it was we were doing—standing there in a curve with rookie drivers roaring by. Dickie came busting into the curve too fast, so fast that he lost control. As Dickie lost control, he grabbed for his hand brakes. That slowed him just enough so that when he hit Grandpa, Grandpa wasn't thrown violently to the ground and run over, but was pushed up on top of the bike, straddling the front tire as he grabbed the handlebars. The only thing that saved Grandpa was that Uncle Richard happened to be standing there, too. He was able to grab a handlebar as it went by and slowed the bike down enough so that Dickie finally got it under control. When Dickie stopped, the sudden lurch threw Grandpa back. He landed on his feet and staggered backwards for some five or six yards before he landed foolishly on his behind. As soon as Grandpa got his breath back and was helped up by many willing and worried hands, he took one look at a horrified Dickie and murmured one cuss word. He turned to Dickie's mom. "I told you he was going to kill somebody on that thing. I just didn't know it would be me!" That broke up the mini-bike riding for that day, but the next day it commenced again. For the rest of the winter and into the early spring, the sounds of mini-bikes could be heard zooming all over the woods, up one trail and down the other. The one time Andy let me ride his bike, I tore out before Dickie and Jimmy and raced for the lake with them in hot pursuit. At the fork in the dirt road, I took the trail that went straight and long behind the lake. They followed, determined to pass me, but Andy's bike was just too fast. I don't know if Dickie forgot where the road ended—didn't know or didn't care—but I went around the last little curve and began slowing down just before the road ended in a dense pine thicket. I instantly realized that Dickie had not throttled back. As he zipped around the curve to find me sitting there waiting, he slammed on his brakes. His back tire locked up, and it started sliding on the years and years of pine straw that had been deposited there. He laid the bike down, and it slid right up to where I was before stopping with Dickie under it. Everything would have been fine, but Jimmy, who had been lagging behind on a smaller and slower bike, now found his full speed and raced around the curve. He found both Dickie and me there, with Dickie crawling out from under his bike. Just before Jimmy crashed into him, I heard Dickie use the same flowery word Grandpa had used when Dickie had nailed him. Once we got everyone untangled and made sure that nobody had gotten killed as Grandpa had predicted, the accusations began to fly. Both boys immediately blamed me for stopping until I pointed out I could go no farther because the road had ended. Then when Dickie saw the dents in his bike, he blamed me for taking that road when I should have gone on down to the lake. I cranked Andy's bike back up and watched as Dickie and Jimmy both tried to crank theirs, but they couldn't. Without a word I rode slowly off, only stopping when I got back to their house to tell Uncle Richard he might want to take the truck down and pick up their bikes because they had crashed them. Grandpa was sitting on the porch and heard our conversation, and I could have sworn I heard him giggle.

The mini-bikes did change the dynamics of the leadership of our group for awhile. I could no longer lead the bicycle expeditions, couldn't outrace the boys to the lake on my bicycle, and couldn't ride up Strawberry Mountain, which they wanted to attempt almost every day. It was early July, and I was talking up a late afternoon baseball game. I had everyone ready to play. Everyone but Dickie that is, who decided that he wanted to ride his mini-bike down to the power line that had been cut through the edge of Grandpa's property. Then he wanted to challenge the others in a contest to see who could ride up Strawberry Mountain first. Strawberry Mountain was the highest elevated hill in the area. It had two tall power line towers sitting on top of it, and its front side had been stripped of all trees, so many motorcycle riders used to have fun riding up it. Dickie was challenging my leadership when he suggested the bike ride, and he knew it. He knew it would cut me out of the activity, which was also fine with him because it would give him a chance to lord his abilities over the younger boys. So instead of baseball, three of the boys of Enon Road ran for their mini-bikes. Soon the air was filled with the roar of them cranking their machines, and the noisy sounds of them barreling down through the woods on the trail to the foot of Strawberry Mountain. Needless to say, I was furious. This was a direct attempt at overthrow, a flagrant unheard of rebellion, and a usurpation of the natural order of life on Enon Road where the oldest boy in the group was always leader. Dickie would get his turn next summer, but he could not wait. Now he led the open rebellion that had to be put down at all costs.

When the boys were cranking their machines, I ran and grabbed my bicycle. It was a hand-me-down Schwinn from my older brother, Travis. It had no fenders, but it did have a well oiled chain that made it fast. Still, it was not nearly fast enough to keep up with the machines. I hit the trail with my bike just behind the boys, and they zoomed off and left me far behind, with Dickie looking back and laughing as he went. His plan couldn't have been going any better. It was a perfect, bloodless coup. Seeing the upper trail that led to the top of the mountain, I pedaled furiously down it as hard as I could go. I soon found myself coming out onto the power line just at the top of Strawberry Mountain, which had an elevation of several hundred feet. Getting to the top, almost out of breath from the exertion, I looked down in time to see Dickie making his first attempt to climb the mountain. Riding recklessly up the trail, he made it three-fourths of the way up before gravity got the better of him and he stopped. But he had set the mark for the other boys to reach. Looking up at me sitting astride my bike, he laughed again and called to me. "Hey. Come on down and let's see how far up the mountain you can go on your bike." Jimmy and Andy thought that was hilarious. Laughing and pointing at me, they made stupid remarks about my bike. They spent about twenty minutes trying to climb that mountain. Finally, after much effort and many attempts, Dickie was the first up. After not too many more attempts, the other boys followed and joined me on top of the hill that had a breathtaking view of Enon Road. Dickie kept making fun of me and my bike and saying I had to try and see how far up the hill I could climb on my piece of junk.

The time to prove my leadership and manhood had come; the time to prove that once and forever I was the rightful leader of the boys of Enon Road; the time to put down this rebellion, this attempted overthrow. "Dickie," I said, "anybody can come up that mountain on one of your bikes. But I haven't ever heard of anyone going down."

They all laughed. "That's because they would be killed," Andy scoffed. "The hill is too steep. These bikes couldn't take it."

"Mine could," I said coldly.

"No way," Dickie answered. "You'd break up. Nobody can do it."

"I'm going to do it on this piece of junk you've been laughing about," I told them. "But I want y'all to go first. You first, Dickie. Your bike is fast. You go down."

"You're crazy," he replied. He looked with fear towards the bottom of the steep hill. "I ain't going down there, and you ain't, neither." I had thrown down the gauntlet in challenge, but he had refused to pick it up.

I pushed my bike up to the very edge. "No," shouted Andy. "If you don't get killed, you'll get busted up bad. You can't do it."

I knew I had to try, even though there was a knot in my stomach. I knew the chances of me surviving were slim, but the idea of spending the rest of the summer riding around behind their mini-bikes with Dickie as their leader was just not appealing to me. "Here goes nothing," I said. "See you girls at the bottom."

With that I pushed off slowly, almost standing on my brakes to keep my speed to a minimum. But it was growing steadily as I moved farther and farther down the hill. I heard Andy's "No!" bellowing in the background, but I was too concerned about staying alive at that point to care. As I reached the halfway point, it was useless to try and keep standing on the brakes. All I could do by then was ride it out the best I could, try to keep the bike from flipping, and try with growing fear to keep the wheels straight. It was a battle. The only time I glanced down at the worn speedometer, it was topping 50 miles per hour. I hit the one hard bump in the trail and went flying high and long through the air, coming down solidly on both wheels and continued my rapid descent. I had expected to be killed on impact or at the least to have my manhood ripped from me because I thought I would slam down on the body of the bike. But the landing was smooth. The boys were paralleling me on the road that ran up the side of the mountain on a more gentle incline, or descent as it was now to them. They tried to keep up with me, but I was moving too fast for them. Finally though, the mountain began to smooth out. I began to slow down and once again regaining control of my speed through the use of the brakes. I coasted to a stop to await the boys. Within a minute they roared up. Turning off their bikes, they all began to talk at once. They pointed up at the mountain, remarked how steep it was, how high it was, looked at me, looked at the bike, and felt the tires to see if they were on fire. They were stunned at what they had just seen. Jimmy and Andy looked at me with wonder and awe.

"Did you see him flying through the air?" Andy exulted. "He must have flown halfway down the mountain. That was great!"

Even Jimmy, Dickie's brother, couldn't believe what he had seen. Dickie had to admit to himself at that point that I was the undisputed leader of the boys of Enon Road. None of the rest of them would even attempt what I had done. Even if they had, they knew that they would not live to tell about it. But I had, and they would tell everyone about it until it became legend; until everyone all over the community heard about it; and until even Mom heard about it at the beauty shop and almost died right there with her hair lathered in shampoo. Not until my son was almost grown would anyone else dare to ride down Strawberry Mountain, but he had heard the legend and challenged it. He would be the one to do it, and he would live up to his dad's record.

But on that day, I was the leader once again. I began

pushing my bike up towards the long trail where it was more level and I could ride back to the house. Just before the boys cranked their bikes, I called out, "Now how about a baseball game?"

"Great," both Jimmy and Andy exclaimed. They were anxious to do anything I suggested—anything except to attempt riding their bikes down that mountain. They drove up the trail and off into the woods, with Dickie dragging along slowly behind them. He was still shaking his head at the extraordinary feat of skill and courage he had just witnessed. He wondered when his time came to be challenged for leadership, if he would have the guts to do something like ride down Strawberry Mountain. After the boys had left, I pushed my bike onto the trail and turned back to look at that mountain one more time. I wondered at how foolish and lucky I had been. I would never try riding down that mountain again.

CHAPTER EIGHTEEN

Deacons and Preachers

U nion Christian Church played an important role in our lives during those early, formative years. Mom and Dad were the main reason, and their influence gradually extended to the Duncans, so much so that Uncle Richard was elected deacon. They never had much luck with Aunt Lois and Uncle Gene. Aunt Lois grew up in a church that taught her that once she was saved, she was always saved, and she could never fall out of God's grace. She didn't see much sense in going to church since she was already saved. She did see to it that her children got to church so they could get saved. Eventually, all her children except for Brad were baptized at Union. He put it off so long that he finally lost the desire to do it. It wasn't until he was as low as a man could get and had contemplated suicide that he finally hit his knees and prayed for the first time in his life.

Union was a friendly little country church in those years. It still met twice on Sunday for worship and then on Wednesday night for prayer meeting and Bible study. It had been a white frame church building in my dad's youth, but his dad's generation had bricked it up in the late 1930s. The pews inside were made of field pine and were hard to sit on. The longer the service went, the harder they got, and the harder they got, the more squirming that went on. There was no air conditioning, not even window units. When revival time came in the dog days of August, the windows would be opened, and the Herschel McDaniel Funeral Home hand fans would be flapping. Moths and wasps would flit from the lights to the pews and back, with an occasional fan used to swat at them. Union did not have a nursery in those days. If a baby out screamed the preacher, then the preacher wasn't considered a very good preacher. During one particularly noisy outbreak of a squalling baby, when the mother stood up to take the baby out, the preacher politely asked her to sit back down and said, "If I can't preach louder than that baby can scream, then I just need to preach harder!" And that was exactly what he did.

Many people have a home church, or a church where they grew up or were baptized. They have a special place like "The Church in the Valley by the Wildwood," a church where they were married or their parents were buried; a church that will always hold a special place in their hearts even years after they have left it. So it is with me and Union Christian. I have so many great memories of that place where the moral force in my life was forged, lesson by lesson, sermon by sermon, revival by revival, VBS by VBS. Mostly I remember the people that were there that one marvelous summer, people that God brought together to influence me and point me and the other boys of Enon Road in the right direction. There was the old deacon, Hoskins Stone, a man with a deep store of wisdom that he was eager to share. Brother Hoskins, as he was called, stood about 6 feet tall, but Daddy said he was taller before he got so old. He was balding on the top but had a rim of thick white hair around the edges. He had huge, strong hands from a lifetime of hard work. About once a year, Brother Hoskins would stand up during church and give his "Little Acorn, What Can You Do?" speech. It was a speech that would motivate us boys and give us hope of growing into someone famous or important. We loved the speech and knew it by heart from having heard it so many times. As big as he was, he was gentle, and we could always depend on an easy pat on the back and an encouraging word from him.

Revival time that summer, and every summer, was the second week in August. That second Sunday was always homecoming. There was dinner on the grounds, where the ladies would bring fried chicken, fresh corn and tomatoes from the garden. Someone would make sure there were gallons of sweet, sweet tea in a washtub with lemons and chunks of ice floating around in it. On the Saturday before, all the men and boys would gather to build the tables on which the mountains of food would sit the next day. We pulled sawhorses out from under the church where they had sat since the last homecoming. We nailed thick plywood to them and set them up under the trees behind the church. We had started at 8:00 am, and it was almost lunchtime. All the tables were almost built when the big, rusty pick-up truck of Brother Hoskins came rolling in with the biggest table we had ever seen lashed to the back. It took five good, hefty men to unload it and set it in place. It was the dessert table, the table that everyone would visit the next day and that some would visit before they even got their main course. We all gathered behind the truck as it was being unloaded. Someone asked Brother Hoskins who had helped him load it. "Just me and Hoskins," he said slowly. "Just me and Hoskins."

Wallace Rice was another man that had a big impact on us boys of Enon Road. He was a deputy sheriff, and legends of his courageous deeds walked before him and lingered after. Wallace was not tall, tended to be pear shaped, and did not look to be a man of immense strength. Rumor was that crooks did not cross him twice, for after the first run in with him, they never wanted to see him again. One time he crawled, by himself, under a house to confront an escaped convict and drug the man out kicking and screaming. That was courage. He was married to a very nice lady, but they never had any children, which was a real shame. Men like that need to pass that kind of courage along. There was a spell there when someone had hurt his feelings at church, or he had gotten mad at the preacher, but for whatever reason he stayed away from church for a long time. He eventually came back more faithful than before, was elected a deacon, and loaned the church the money to build the new Sunday school rooms that were needed so badly. Wallace—or just Mr. Rice, as we called him—was a good man, truthful, and hard working. He was the kind of man we boys respected and feared. His one weakness was that he was prejudiced against black people. Maybe it was the era he was raised in, or maybe his parents were that way—I don't know. But I do know that stories got out that it was he that had told the church board that they needed to be ready when a black person tried to come to church. If it happened on a day that he was there, he would personally escort him out. To Mr. Rice, whites had their churches and they did not go to the black churches; the blacks had their churches and should not bother the white churches. He called them "negras" and did not believe in the mixing of the races in restaurants, schools, and especially not in churches. It was ironic that when he died, the first black people ever to come to the church were the ones that attended his funeral. Sitting in the Amen corner was an honor guard of six black deputies in full dress uniform. They would escort him to his grave. We boys of Enon Road heard the adults talking about it in wonder, and one of them made the comment with a laugh, "I bet old Wallace was turning over in his coffin with those black deputies there." We didn't understand the humor, but we laughed anyway.

The man with the biggest impact was the preacher at Union in those years, Brother Joshua Storey. He was a retired preacher/farmer or farmer/preacher who came out of preaching retirement to fill the pulpit at Union after a nasty church fight, which concluded with that preacher and a few of his followers leaving. Brother Storey was going to fill in until a new preacher was found, but the board showed no inclination towards finding another preacher, so it was five more years before he finally retired again. He stood about 5'9" tall, was short and as rotund as a good old minister should be. By the summer of 1968, he was into this third year with us, and we had heard all his stories and examples in his sermons at least three or four times. We knew all about every deathbed conversion he had attended, every dramatic baptism he had participated in, every church he had ever served, and all the people in those churches and the spirit filled lives they lived. What we did not realize then was that in his wisdom, he understood that repetition is a great form of teaching and learning. Years later, we still remember his illustrations and the points he made. One thing he said was, "If all you can do in the Lord's service is to shake people into church and shake their hands going out, then you had better get to shaking."

The boys of Enon Road loved the man because he had baptized, or would eventually baptize, every one of us except Brad. Two weeks before revival that year, he called us boys up after church. He told us that he needed some help putting revival advertisement flyers in mailboxes around the community and asked if we would help. We would start early and be done by noon. Afterwards he would take us all over to Cook's store on the corner of Pitman and Stonewall Tell and let us reach way down into Mr. Cook's ice cold refrigerator and pull out whatever type "belly washer" we wanted. (Having just returned from several years in Chicago not too long before, Little Dickie called the drinks "pop." It was such a Yankee term that we were ashamed of him for a long time after that. We always just said, "You wanna Coke?" and by that we meant any kind of carbonated beverage.) With that kind of enticement, we all readily agreed to go. Braving Mr. Storey's well known erratic driving, we spent one Saturday morning going all over the community and putting flyers in every mailbox. In those days you could still put your flyers in mailboxes because no one had yet declared the doctrine that the mailboxes belonged to the post office and could only hold official United States Post Office mail. We never could figure out how our parents had to buy the mailbox, put the mailbox up, and maintain the mailbox, but the government could tell what you could and could not have delivered to it. That same government had not even spent a dime on that mailbox.

By noon, the four of us that were helping were ready for our "pop," and Brother Storey was ready to get home to his lunch. He pulled that big white Buick of his into the small, dusty parking lot of that store. We all piled out and ran into the store, with the screen door banging behind us, of course. Sliding the metal door back on the drink box, we peered down into the gloom and felt like we were diving for buried treasure. I reached in first and pulled out an Orange Crush. Little Dickie made everybody mad by taking so long. He pulled out drink after drink and put them back before finally deciding on a Kickapoo Joy Juice, a lemon-lime flavored drink. Andy was with us, and he went for the Redrock Cola, a cola that left a hot sting in your throat. Brad pulled out a Barley Chocolate drink. Mr. Storey did not even look. He just stuck his hand way down deep and pulled out a Nugrape soda. Mr. Cook was sitting behind the counter with the usual staff of two or three fellas hanging around with nothing better to do. He was laughing at us and our excitement over getting something as simple as a cold drink. We stood around the store, wandering around and eyeing all the candies and cookies and various types of tobacco until we finished with our drinks. As we left, we noticed that Mr. Cook was posting our revival flyer on his window, and that made us proud.

The thing about Mr. Storey was that he was as faithful a servant of his God as you could find. He practiced what he preached and preached what he practiced. He was a man faithful to God, church, wife, and family. Years later, one grandson became the president of a Christian college and several other sons, sons-in-law, and grandsons became ministers. Oddly enough, my daughter met Mr. Storey's great-great nephew in college and married him. Yes, he definitely made an impact on us—not with just what he said, but how he lived.

CHAPTER NINETEEN

⇒ *Muscadine Vines* ⇐

With the coming of revival, we knew that the summer was almost over, that school would soon be back in session, and that those long evenings of playing ball were almost gone. But there were still some exciting times left, and one of those was the annual "gathering of muscadines." When Grandpa had first walked over that property as a young man considering buying it, he found a land that was rich, much like the twelve Israelite spies had found Canaan. It had several creeks and streams, two of which he later dammed to make the lake that he stocked with fish. There was an abundance of pastureland where he would be able to graze cattle, and there was already a barn. All over the property were cedar trees, and I wonder if Grandpa ever imagined the fun we would have for so many years in hunting Christmas trees. It became an annual rite of Christmas for us. He loved to stand out by the gate when we drug our tree proudly by him. Every year he jokingly measured it, saying, "This one is gonna cost you a bunch because I charge by the foot, you know!" I don't know who was prouder of those Christmas trees, Grandpa or us.

There were also lots of wild plum bushes dotting the landscape. We used to gather those red and yellow plums for Grandma from time to time so she could make plum jelly. One day we found a tree with a different kind of fruit way up high. After knocking one out with a rock, we coaxed Larry into tasting it. From the terrible expression on Larry's face when he bit into it, we learned that green persimmons were not something we needed to eat. Another tree grew low to the ground and had a fruit that looked like a cross between a softball and an orange. We called it a "mock orange" tree, which we have since learned is an Osage orange, but we never found out if its fruit was good for anything. It always fell off and rotted under the tree. We harvested black walnuts, too, and would store them in the loft of the barn in a burlap bag.

Grandpa had also found a land that grew lots and lots of muscadines. I don't know if God planted them at creation, or if some family from years long since past had planted them, or how they had grown, but there were several large trees that were covered with muscadine vines. The biggest of these was at the end of the road to the lake, just before you drove into the clearing at the water's edge. It was a family event, the gathering of muscadines. The adults walked, and the kids rode in the back of the light green truck, one of two Grandpa used in his electrical business. It was the one with a homemade roof covering the bed. The dogs usually ran behind nipping at the truck tires, except for Tiger, who joyfully rode in the back with us jostling, pushing, and hollering boys. The truck pulled up under the tree by a long limb that stretched out over the dirt road. My two younger uncles would stand on top of the truck and climb up onto that limb. They would work their way back to the base of the tree, then straight up from limb to limb. The muscadine vines hung thick all around them, so when they got as far up as the fruit was, they began to shake the vines. It literally rained muscadines on our heads as we waited below for the round, purple fruit to fall. We stood there with paper grocery bags opened and made a game of catching as many in the bag as we could. Grandpa sat in the truck watching happily and laughing. The uncles worked their way down the tree and out onto the limbs to shake as much down as they could. When they were finally finished, we all began to pick up as much as we could without stepping on any. But by the end of the day, our tennis shoe bottoms would be purple with the juice of smashed muscadines. The adults got in on the act, too, filling as many bags as they could so that before long we had most of the muscadine crop harvested. Since the adults dreaded the walk back up the hill towards the houses, everyone including the dogs packed into the back of the truck with the bags of fruit. The younger uncles stretched out on the roof and held on for dear life, while several of the dads sat on the let-down tailgate with their feet dragging the ground behind the truck as it struggled up the hill.

Our work was over but the women's work was just beginning, especially Grandma's. She set out to make as much jelly as she possibly could. She made enough to get us through that winter (and several winters to come) and enough to give away to relatives or to sell for the school at the fall carnival. I don't how she did it, but when she was finished, she had lots and lots of jars of all kinds full of jelly, all sealed with hardened wax. There were no lids, just wax. I believe that if any of that jelly had survived till today under all that wax, it would still be as fresh as when Grandma made it.

I don't know it for a fact, but I do believe that Grandma may have made some muscadine wine out of

145

what was left over. It was wine for "medicinal purposes." The Apostle Paul in the Bible did tell his disciple Timothy that a little wine was good for the stomach, so it must have been all right with God if Grandma kept some stashed in the refrigerator. It was safely out of reach of the grandkids and was to be brought out only for emergency situations like when Paregoric or enemas did not work. I asked Little Dickie one time if he had ever been dosed with the wine. All he said was, "If you have the choice between the wine and an enema, take the enema."

CHAPTER TWENTY

⋙ *Moby Strikes* ⋘

Summer vacation was almost over. School started back on Monday, and we had already visited J.C. Penny's at Greenbriar Mall and bought our new jeans and tennis shoes. The jeans would still be tight and made you walk like a zombie when you put them on. They would be dark blue, not faded, and they would not have patches on the knees. We appreciated getting them, even if they were stiff. Summer had been busy from start to finish, every day packed with activity. Now we had to get back in the school routine. For me it would be a year where I would be in the seventh grade and would get to take the school's annual Safety Patrol trip to Washington. On Monday morning we would be decked out in our new jeans, shoes, and new shirts, and we would stand up at the end of the driveway to wait for the bus. We would be holding our Blue Horse notebooks, the ones where you could cut out the Blue Horse head symbol, save it with tens of thousands of others, and then send them in for neat prizes like bikes or bubblegum, depending on how many you had. There we would wait on the school bus with a mixture of excitement and fear. No more sleeping in. No more getting up late and watching cartoons. No more ballgames in the afternoons. Now our afternoons would be full of reports, homework, and studying.

Our last Friday before school started back was busy,

as we were determined to cram every thing into it that we could. We rode bikes, played in the woods, built a new hut, played army, and that was all before lunch. After lunch we played our final baseball game of the season. One of our unwritten rules was that front yard ball ended when school started. Soon after that, the old football would be pulled out and we put away the ball gloves and bats until next summer. There was nothing spectacular about that last game that year, not even with us knowing that it was likely my last game ever. I don't even remember now who won. I do know that I never hit one over the road and don't know if I could do it today. The Bambino was the only one of our gang to ever do it, and he only did it that one time.

My greatest disappointment that summer, even greater than the promised ball field not being built, was that I had not tangled with "The Grandpa" despite all the hours I had spent at the lake. Despite all the casts I had made, all the sunburns I had gotten, and all the mosquito bites I had suffered while fishing in the dark, the great fish had never approached my bait. I had caught lots of bass, mostly smaller ones that kept fishing interesting. But in the back of my mind, I wanted to catch that great monster that still lurked somewhere in that lake. I would be a man soon, and if I could somehow catch that fish, it would prove to the world that I was a man. Now with school starting and fall approaching swiftly, my time was running out. On that last Saturday before school started, I made plans to go fishing one last time.

It was late August and still hot and sultry, so I decided to go to the lake after supper that evening. To pass the time until then, I went with Dad over to the church and cut the grass in the church cemetery. I was always on the lookout for wasps or those dreaded yellow jackets that built nests in the ground. They would lay in wait until you and the mower had passed over the nest before attacking you from the rear. We went over to Papa's on Butner Road, too, but the watermelon patch did not have any more melons left, just some old rotting little knots that had never made much.

Finally we returned home, and Mom had supper on the table: fried salmon patties and cold pork and beans right out of the can. I can still smell the kitchen full of the aroma of that sizzling salmon, and I can taste those patties. After supper, I gathered my gear. With a quick word to the folks and their usual word of caution in return, I hiked down to the lake. Luckily no one else was there using the boat, so I would have the lake to myself. Turning the boat over gently with a quick look for snakes, I pushed it out into the water. After loading it with my equipment, I climbed in. As the boat gently moved away from the shore, I took a quick stock of the conditions. There was almost no wind. The lake was up and just a little muddy. The sky was mostly clear with little chance of rain, and I could hear some fish already jumping around the edges. The conditions were perfect.

Paddling down to the deep end, I began throwing my pink jelly worm towards the shore and dragging it back to the boat. Working my way up the bank towards the cattails, I kept a throwing distance away from the shore. About halfway up the dam, I hooked a little bass, and after a brief struggle put him in the boat. But not before he danced on the top of that water. I always loved to see the fish dance. Throwing him back, I put the boat

back in position and kept fishing. Getting close to the cattails, I put one cast right in the front. I sat there holding
my breath, praying to God to make that fish grab it, but
nothing happened. After five or six more disappointing
casts, I paddled down towards the shallow end of the lake
and fished among the stumps and logs. I caught two more
little fish and lost one bigger one when he spit the hook
out, but no Moby Bass.

As I sat there fishing, I thought a lot about the past,
about all the fun we had that summer, and about how my
days of hut building and playing army would soon be over.
Before long, adult things would demand my attention,
and though I hated to admit it, I might even start to get
interested in girls. The next fall I would start high school
and would be a teenager. I would get pimples, grow really
fast, and start dreaming of having my own car.

A gentle tug on my line snapped me back to reality.
I watched it pull off, and then I reeled up to it and set back
on the hook. Once again a small bass broke the plane of
the lake and danced in the sky before settling back into
the water. I got him in the boat and as with the others,
turned him loose. It was beginning to get late. Already the
light was starting to fade, and the first bats had made their
swooping appearance. The nightly call of the frogs began.
That usually was my sign to head for home, but on this
night I wanted one last shot at Moby Bass. Reaching into
my front shirt pocket, I pulled out the black flip-tail plastic worm that I had been saving for this occasion. I had
found it two days earlier while cleaning out my grandpa's
tackle box. It might have been a mate of the worm that my
dad had used when he hooked that giant fish, or it could
have been the very worm itself. It was marked and slightly

torn. Carefully putting it on my hook, I then picked up the paddle and stroked through the darkening shadows to the deep. I let the boat glide into place some distance away from the cattails, then I made a cast towards those same cattails. There was a little bush sticking up about three yards in front of them, and my worm landed just to the side of it. It was too dark to see the line, but as I began to reel it in, I felt a very gentle tap or tug, maybe caused by the worm hanging on that bush. I pulled back quickly to get it off the bush when suddenly it pulled back hard, almost jerking the rod from my hands.

I had never felt anything that hard pulling against me, and it was all I could do to hang on. Could it be? Was it? With dark coming fast, did I finally have the legendary fish on my line? It could be dangerous. I was not a powerful swimmer, and if the boat were to tip over in the struggle, I was sure to drown. I tried to reel, but the fish was too big and the reel too small. So nothing happened, turn though I might. The bass was not moving but was just sitting there, thinking. Finally, I noticed the boat begin to move. It actually sailed noiselessly towards the middle of the lake. The Grandpa was pulling the boat to the deepest water where he would destroy me. I felt like Captain Ahab in pursuit of Moby Dick, and I remembered how that movie with Gregory Peck had ended. Fear shot through me as the boat moved slowly through the water. A thought came to cut the line, but I shook my head and waited hopefully for the great fish to tire.

In the distance, I saw a flash of lightning and heard a muffled roll of thunder. A surprise evening storm was rushing in from Alabama. Not now. Not tonight when I was finally, after so many fruitless attempts, doing combat with my archenemy. Darkness was settling in, and I knew I was due home right at that moment. I could almost hear Mom's voice calling me from far, far away. A car horn was blowing in the distance, a noise that was Mom's call to come home immediately. I was finally able to reel the fish in for a few inches, but he soon stripped it back off as he reached the deep water and tried to dive even deeper. I held on, and the good old Zebco reel finally stopped whining and made its last stand, not letting out any more line. Pulling back and keeping the rod tip up, I managed to keep that fish from going down and wrapping the line around some deeply submerged limb as he obviously intended. Frustrated, the mighty fish pulled harder and swam towards the shallow end of the lake. This was dangerous for a fish his size, but it also afforded him more cover to tangle the line.

A few drops of rain fell, and I heard them splatter on the floor of the boat. I realized with the next lightning flash that it was dark. Was I ever in trouble when I got home! The storm rumbled ever nearer and would soon be right on top of me. To cause me even more trouble, the wind had picked up and was trying to blow me off the lake, but only that fish kept me in the water. Suddenly I understood what the mammoth was doing. He was going to the same spot where Mr. Wilson claimed to have lost him so many years earlier. I knew then that Mr. Wilson had fought this same whale, and if I did not do something quick, the outcome would be the same. Once again summoning the Zebco, I turned the crank and felt even more give as the tiring fish slowly began to fade. Raindrops were pelting down my back. I was oblivious to the rain and the storm that could kill me at any minute; I thought of nothing but hanging on. A blast of wind hit the boat broad side and almost flipped it over. The blast turned the boat around, which threatened to hit the line and break it. I had to stand up quickly and hold the line high as the boat swung under it. I sat down quickly so I would not fall over.

A tremendous crack of lightning blasted a tree down at the dam. I could smell the air and knew it was a pine that had been hit. That was too close. As much as I wanted it, as close as I was, this fish was not worth my life. Besides, I had already fought him to a draw—a dead even stand still—keeping him from using all his little tricks to break the line. Yet try as I might to get him to the boat, he tried harder to keep away from it. Try as he might to get away, I tried harder to beat him. Finally, with pain shooting up my back from the fight, and with my arms feeling numb, I reached down and felt for the tackle box. Finding it, I flipped it open and reached for the knife. In the next lightning flash I saw it and pulled it out, getting it ready to cut the line.

Looking out at the water, in the next tremendous flash of lightning I saw something I never dreamed I would see. That mighty fish of legend, the Grandpa, Moby Bass himself, had risen from the depths. In a last gasp, desperate surge for life and freedom, the leviathan crashed through the water into the storm stricken atmosphere. I stared in horror at his size as I saw what was left of my worm hanging from his mouth. He was huge; a giant; the largest bass I had ever seen, and far larger than I had imagined even in my dreams. Soaring into the rain, he shook his head wickedly. I felt like Captain Ahab ready to throw a harpoon into him, except I remembered once again how

Ahab had ended. The fish smashed back down into the water with a terrifying smack that was louder than even the thunder and the pounding rain. Once again lightning lit the sky. Once again the creature of the lake danced on the water, twisting this way and that. Once again the huge fish smacked into the water with a tremendous splash.

I had seen enough. No one would ever believe me, but the moment had come, and I knew what I had to do. With one quick movement, the knife hit the line, and the pole shot straight up into the air. It flapped crazily for some seconds. The releasing tension also shot the boat back, and I was afraid it was would crash into the trees. Grabbing the paddle, I got my bearings as to where the boat landing was. I then paddled against that wind and rain with the little remaining strength that I had. I was about half way to where I hoped the shore was when I heard a truck coming and saw lights moving quickly down the road. The lights swayed from to side as the vehicle slid in what must have been a muddy torrent. If there ever was a frog strangler, that was it. I realized at that moment that I should have let that fish kill me because since it hadn't, whoever was coming in that truck to look for me would.

Still struggling against the wind, I saw the old, green Chevrolet Apache truck pull right down to the water's edge. Its headlights played out on the water and picked me up in its beam. Dad and Grandpa piled out into the rain with no hats, no rain gear, and no umbrellas. Daddy slumped against the truck momentarily. Relief that they weren't finding my lifeless body made his legs suddenly weak now that the adrenalin had drained away. Grandpa grabbed his flashlight from the cab and shown it out on the lake, too, as I rowed ever closer against the wind. Almost out of strength, I had to stop paddling about fifteen yards from shore. It was then that Dad finally found his legs and came running into the water to help. The water was waist deep when he reached me, and was I ever glad to feel his arms take the end of that boat and pull it towards shore. I dropped the paddle and just bowed over as if in prayer. I was so tired and drained.

Dad was behind the boat. He pushed me up to the bank, where Grandpa grabbed the end of the boat and pulled it up partway onto shore. Rushing down the boat to me, he got there before Dad could wade his way out of the lake. I heard Grandpa's relieved but angry voice. "What in the world were you doing out there? You could have been killed! You got your momma all tore up and worried." He said a few more choice words that Momma would have been ashamed to hear him say, but given the stress of the situation, I am sure she would have forgiven him. I felt his hand on my back, comforting me as Dad finally worked his way out of the dark water.

"Are you all right, son?" were his still frightened words.

Finally taking a deep breath, I looked up into his and Grandpa's eyes. "It was him. I had the Grandpa! I saw him and had to cut him loose before I got killed."

Grandpa looked at Dad, and Dad looked at him as if they suddenly understood; for they had been in that same boat years before fighting that same leviathan. Another flash of lightning prevented any more discussion. Leaving my rifle and all the other equipment, they hustled me to the truck where I climbed in beside them. Grandpa cranked the truck, backed it up, and we began the wild ride home through the mud. Little raging rivers washed gullies (and strangled unfortunate frogs) in the road as the headlights picked them out. Grandpa always managed to find the solid, high ground. So despite slipping and spinning a few times, we finally were roaring by the black walnut tree and then out of the trees where the sky was suddenly lighter. We roared by the barn and the mulberry tree, through the gate, and into Grandpa's yard where he sat down on his horn.

People came swirling out of the house, with my mom in the lead. Before my feet had hit the ground I was in her arms. She was hugging me and we were both crying, standing there in the rain. Little Dickie was there, and he was crying, too. Grandma scurried out and shooed everyone in out of the rain. She immediately covered me and Grandpa and Dad with towels. We were all soaked to the skin and dripped water all over Grandma's floor, but she did not seem to mind.

It wasn't long before Grandma had a pot of milk on the stove to make some hot chocolate. She always said that something hot inside would help knock off the chill outside. I was just glad she wasn't pulling out the muscadine wine. Grandpa and Daddy rehearsed their rescue for everyone as I sat at the kitchen table. I was cuddled up next to Mom with a towel around me. Finally all eyes turned to me for an explanation as to how I could have been so foolish.

"I hooked the Grandpa," I said simply. There was an intake of breath around the table. "I had him, but it got dark and the storm hit. Lightning hit a tree on the dam, and I had to cut him loose."

Some looked at me with awe, others with skepticism. "I know because I saw it dance. Twice, right before I had to cut him loose. It was the biggest fish I ever saw."

From there I gave them a cast by cast review of my evening. Grandpa shook his gray head up and down in acknowledgement that he knew what I was saying was true. Finally, after all the questions were answered, we were able to relax and enjoy the chocolate. It was good. I noticed that the boys of Enon Road held me in awe and treated me almost reverentially. It was a good feeling.

The storm had passed and the rain had ended when we finally got up to go home. I was so tired I could barely stand, but Mom put her arm around me and escorted me to the door. Just as I was leaving, Grandpa walked over and called me. He put out his hand. I took it, knowing in that moment that he was seeing me not only as a grandson, but as a man.

CHAPTER TWENTY ONE

➢ *Innocence* ⤜

W here did those days go? I want them back. I want
to ride that bicycle down that road again in the
mid-day sun with nothing in front of me but miles of level
road with open pasture on both sides. I want to play baseball in that yard just one more time with all the boys. I
want to hit just one homerun over that road, circling those
bases with my fist pumping the air as Dickie frets on the
mound. I want to fight those wars in the woods again,
against the unseen, imaginary, but very real to us enemy. I
want to fish in that lake once more and battle that legendary bass. I want to fish there with Grandpa, and this time I
want to paddle the boat all around the lake and just watch
him fish and learn from him. And yes, I even want to cut
Aunt Alma's yard again just so I can stand under that old
elm tree and drink that ice cold Coke. I can almost taste
its icy sweetness now, years later, just thinking about it.
I want to milk that cow with Grandma one more time,
hearing that milk go splat, splat, splash in the bucket. I
want to go over to her house and go through that closet
under the stairs where all the old helmets and hats were.
I want to wear them once more, dreaming I am a cop, or
a soldier. I want to go to Papa's and eat watermelon with
him on Sunday afternoons after worship service. I want
to go back to that little church and find something I have
lost in the years since I have left. If I can't find my inno-

cence there, maybe I can find something else like forgive-
ness. Or maybe even I can find God again, the powerful
God I knew as a kid; the God who could and would do
anything for the people he loved. Somewhere in the ensuing years I have lost that picture of God, but deep down I
know he is still there and that he still cares. I want to find
him again.

I want to see Momma again as the young woman
that laid down with me for my afternoon naps. I want to
hear her exciting stories, legends, and fables. I want to see
the young woman with the strong arms and wide smile
that won my dad's heart. I want her to be able to see well
and to hear well, and I want to taste her deviled egg sandwiches that she made especially for me without the pick-
les in them. I want to stand out in the yard with Daddy
and let him hit fly balls like he used to do on Saturday
afternoons. I want to go down to the woodshed with him
and help him get in the wood for the evening fire. I want
to go back, back to Enon Road in 1968, and stay there forever. The Bible says heaven will be a place where there will
be no pain or crying or death, kind of like Enon Road was
for us. I wonder if there will be a road in Heaven called
Enon Road. It was a haven, a safe place; a place where we
were safe from aging, from old age pains, and from fear
of illness. It was a place where we were safe from worries
over the kids and from worries over the bills that have to
be paid. We were safe from not being able to sleep more
than three or four hours a night, and safe from wondering
when and why I started snoring. The boys of Enon Road
did not have those worries in 1968.

But those days are gone. They are over. The innocence of those idyllic days has passed, never to be lived

again. I know now how really wicked people can be, as I have seen the blood stains of a murdered friend on her bedroom floor. I have been to the cemetery and funeral home far too many times for both young and old, but not for any of the boys of Enon Road—not yet. I have learned a lot about life since 1968. I learned how much pain being in love can be as I loved and lost in love. I know what stress can do to you when you can't meet the deadlines at work. I know now that good friends can betray you and stab you in the back, and that people you thought you could trust will often do something that will disappoint you or let you down. I have lost that innocence through the ensuing years. While not bitter, I am jaded, and I continue to mourn the loss of my innocence.

With my aging came the changes in my body that I thought would never come when I was back on Enon Road. Where I could see for miles, now I have to wear glasses and struggle to see even with them on. Where I could run forever, now I am out of breath just walking to the mailbox. I don't play ball anymore. I hurt when I get out of bed in the morning, and now my wife tells me that my hair is starting to turn gray. But that is fine, she says, because it is not starting to turn loose—a gene I must have inherited from my grandpa. I think more about taking vitamins now, drinking juice, and eating fiber and vegetables—things I never considered on Enon Road. Then it was hamburgers and hotdogs and Cokes and cakes and pie and ice cream. We had never heard of cholesterol, cancer, high blood pressure, or diabetes. I go to the doctor now for yearly physicals, always thankful when he finds nothing wrong and sees no need for further tests.

Even Enon Road itself is finally changing. Grandma

and Grandpa lay side by side in the old church graveyard. Papa lays there with Nanny, as do many other saints and sinners I have known through the years. Most of the old preachers, VBS teachers, and deacons are dead now or spending their last days in nursing homes. The old barn is gone, having burned in the late 1980s. The property that Grandpa walked over as a young man and bought for his family and their kids and their kids has changed hands several times. Now the lake has been drained and refilled, and all the generations of all the fish we ever caught are gone. Neither Moby Bass nor his offspring are there anymore. A golf course covers most of the property where we used to hunt Christmas trees, let our dogs run, and take walks with the kids. The rest of the property is now a subdivision. Somehow we have let developers convince us that we are not making progress unless we are cutting down trees, building homes, apartments, and businesses. We are not making progress, developers say, unless we are bringing in more and more people and more kids than the schools can hold. If we are not building new roads and widening the old ones; if the old two-lane, tar road where you could ride your bike and never see a car is not four lanes with traffic lights every three or four blocks, then you have not made progress. For me, progress is having the desire and wisdom to let everything stay as it is without worrying about enlarging your tax base. Progress is learning that you don't have to change things or tear things down. Sometimes people like things just the way they are and don't want subdivisions where the cow pastures used to be. Sadly, all this progress is enveloping Enon Road.

The mulberry tree is long gone, having burned when the barn did. It smoked like a chimney for days because it was hollow inside. The old oak that had the muscadines is still standing thanks to a county ordinance preserving all trees of a certain size, but it is sick and dying. The trailer where Grandma lived with her Chihuahua, Jocko, after Grandpa died is long gone. Now that piece of property is for sale at a ridiculously high price, and yet people come by daily to see it. Nothing stays the same forever, even as much as we want it to. Even the old, black Baptist church that has stood for over a century at the corner of Enon and Stonewall has built a new, big sanctuary across the street. Enon Road is changing—the place where I last had that innocence that I so desperately want back.

The boys of Enon Road are different, too. Dickie is pushing 50, making a living designing computer games about wars in space. He never hit a growth spurt in his teenage years and grew out rather than up. Now Dickie is nearly 230 lbs, balding, has had heart surgery twice, but is happily married with three grown children. Stevie is still living on the old home place, a throwback to the age when we were kids. He never changed, except that now there is no one to see his fits or respond to them. Stevie lives by himself and seems supremely happy being exactly who he is. Their bother, Jimmy, moved to Kansas, married a farm girl, inherited her dad's farm, and now works from sunup to sundown. Poor Brad has struggled from job to job and marriage to marriage. But now he is not only fighting alcoholism but also cancer. He is a shadow of his former self. My younger brother, Andy, is wrinkling around the eyes, losing hair, and recently remarked that when he looks in the mirror, he sees our dad. Life has a way of wearing you down.

I have searched for that innocence ever since I left

Enon Road. I have grieved over the loss of it. I have desperately wanted to be back on Enon Road, my own town of Mayberry like the TV show. One day I realized that many people want to find a town like Mayberry, or a place like Enon Road, but Mayberry and Enon Road aren't places as much as they are moments in time; moments before the sin and evil in the world overwhelm us. They are moments in time when we live simpler, easier, less stressed lives. They are moments of innocence and tranquility.

I will never personally know innocence again this side of heaven, but I found innocence in others. I found it in the shining eyes of the very young in every generation. For with every generation there is new hope that things will be better, will turn out differently. In every generation there are the young who have not been exposed to the cares and troubles of the world. Yes, innocence lives on. I found it in my children and hope to find it in theirs one day. Despite all the decadence on television and despite all the moral filth so easily available, our young children still maintain their age of innocence for at least a little while longer. They still want to hold our hands when we walk in the backyard late in the evening, and at night they still want to lie beside us in bed as they drift off to sleep. They want us to kneel beside their beds and listen to their prayers, and they want to hear us pray for them. They are not ashamed to be seen with us in the store, and they eagerly sit beside us on the sofa as we watch football games together. They can jump into our laps and tell us, "Daddy, I love you," or maybe one day soon, "Grandpa, I love you." I still remember looking into the angelic face of my young son as those tender eyes gazed up at me from under that head of blond hair. I saw myself. Once again

I was innocent; once again I was back with the boys of Enon Road. Then I remember Pandora's box had one thing left in it after all the evil had escaped into the world. There was hope.

TATE PUBLISHING & *Enterprises*

Tate Publishing is commited to excellence in the publishing industry. Our staff of highly trained professionals, including editors, graphic designers, and marketing personnel, work together to produce the very finest books available. The company reflects the philosophy established by the founders, based on Psalms 68:11,

"THE LORD GAVE THE WORD AND GREAT WAS THE COMPANY OF THOSE WHO PUBLISHED IT."

If you would like further information, please call
1.888.361.9473
or visit our website
www.tatepublishing.com

TATE PUBLISHING & *Enterprises*, LLC
127 E. Trade Center Terrace
Mustang, Oklahoma 73064 USA